Leading Systems

BARRY OSHRY

LEADING SYSTEMS

LESSONS FROM THE POWER LAB

Berrett-Koehler Publishers, Inc.
San Francisco

Berrett-Koehler Publishers, Inc.
450 Sansome Street, Suite 1200
San Francisco, CA 94111-3320
Tel: (415)288-0260   Fax: (415)362-2512   www.bkconnection.com

ORDERING INFORMATION

Quantity sales. Special discounts are available on quantity purchases by corporations, associations, and others. For details, contact the "Special Sales Department" at the Berrett-Koehler address above.

Individual sales. Berrett-Koehler publications are available through most bookstores. They can also be ordered direct from Berrett-Koehler: Tel: (800) 929-2929; Fax: (802) 864-7626; www.bkconnection.com

Orders for college textbook/course adoption use. Please contact Berrett-Koehler: Tel: (800) 929-2929; Fax: (802) 864-7626.

Orders by U.S. trade bookstores and wholesalers. Please contact Publishers Group West, 1700 Fourth Street, Berkeley, CA 94710. Tel: (510) 528-1444; Fax (510) 528-3444.

 Printed in the United States of America
Printed on acid-free and recycled paper that is composed of 50% recovered fiber, including 10% post consumer waste.

Library of Congress Cataloging-in-Publication Data

Oshry, Barry, 1932-
    Leading systems : lessons from the Power Lab / Barry Oshry.
      p.   cm.
    Includes bibliographical references and index.
    ISBN 1-57675-072-8 (alk. paper)
    1. Social systems. 2. Leadership. 3. Power (Social sciences)
I. Title.
HM701.O85   1999
306—dc21   99-34616
                                         CIP

First Edition
  05 04 03 02 01 00 99   10 9 8 7 6 5 4 3 2 1
Cover designed by Richard Adelson
Text designed by Greene Design

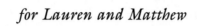

for Lauren and Matthew

I discovered recently that the philosopher Baruch Spinoza once said he was less interested in changing the world than in merely understanding it. For many years that has also been my quest. Yet I am convinced that Spinoza and I share the belief that with deep understanding the world cannot help but change.

—*Barry Oshry*

I have looked at what the universe has shown, to bear witness to it through my paintbrush. Put your hand in mine and let us help one another see things better.

—*Claude Monet*

C O N T E N T S

ACKNOWLEDGMENTS

The Power Lab was born at a time when it was taboo to even talk about power in most corporate settings; power simply did not exist, and the Lab would not have survived those early years if it weren't for the support of Warner Burke and Vlad Dupre at the National Training Laboratories. I am grateful for the contributions of the many staff members who worked with us in the early Power Labs as we struggled to shape this often unruly experience into a coherent educational event: Nancy Lynn Brown, Rob Daly, Joe Luft, and Fritz Steele. In later years we were assisted by Carolyn Carder, Lynda Detterman, Judy Nast-Cole, Neil Kutzen, and Peter Stroh. I am particularly grateful to the current staff of the Power Lab whose commitment to participants and to one another breathes real meaning into such terms as high-performance teams and robust systems: Jane Critchlow, Marcia Hyatt, Anne Litwin, Joe Meier, Mary Lou Michael, Jonathan Milton, Phil Novick, Kevin Purcell, Bob Rehm, Michael Sales, and Joan Wofford. My thanks to Frank Basler, Neila Hingorani, Stewart Lanier, Jeff Pym, and Christi Olson, whose critical readings of early drafts pushed me to deepen and clarify my thinking. I am grateful to my long-time colleague Joe Meier (again) for the many powerful contributions he has made to the Power Lab as both staff member and participant, and for his work in creating the Terrible Dance of Power web site. I am appreciative of my partnership with Bill Woodson and Anne Litwin (again) in the development of the Creating Community in the Face of Difference workshop, and of Anne's generosity in allowing me to use her "I"/"US" Identity exercise in this work. Thanks to Erik Taros of EAT Design for cleaning up my hand-drawn figures and making them computer friendly, to Elissa Rabellino for saving me from embarrassing grammatical errors, to my cherished publisher, Steven Piersanti, who relentlessly urges me on to ever deeper levels of exploration, to the hundreds of adventurous learners who have journeyed into the Power Lab and enabled all of us to learn and grow together, to the staff of the Craigville Conference Center—housekeeping, kitchen, grounds, the front office—who have become our valued partners in creating a magical space in which the Power Lab can flourish. And finally there is one spirit who moves through all of this history—from our earliest struggles in the wilderness, through the evolution of the Power Lab over these thirty years, through all of the writings about power and system life, including more drafts of this current work than any human should be asked to endure; and that spirit is my wife and partner, Karen Ellis Oshry, without whose continuous contributions and inspiration none of this would have happened. I thank you all.

Barry Oshry
Boston, Massachusetts

P R O L O G U E :

◊

Ants, Termites, Bees, and Us

I have spent much of my professional life chasing a single question: Can we humans see the human systems of which we are a part?

We humans look with awe at the remarkable system accomplishments of such creatures as ants and bees and termites—thousands of tiny creatures working together, communicating, their differentiated responsibilities all coming together in the service of the Hill, the Hive. Yet their accomplishments, as amazing as they are, are dwarfed by our own. We humans are the most social of all creatures, and the accomplishments of our systems are truly astounding: the products they make, the services they provide, the food they produce, the art they create, the knowledge they generate, the technology they develop. Yet early on in my work I noticed a peculiar paradox. Human systems—organizations, families, nations—in addition to their amazing accomplishments, persist in living out self-limiting and often destructive stories; but members within these systems do not experience themselves as living out any familiar story. Members do not wake in the morning and say, "Hey gang, I've got a good idea, why don't we just re-create the same old destructive story?" Instead, they simply rise, go about their business, do what they do—and then the familiar story happens.

And when the destructive consequences of these familiar stories occur—breakdowns in relationships, disintegration of systems, turf wars, cold wars, ethnic wars, and culture wars—members attribute these consequences to their particular circumstances, to the personal characteristics of the individuals involved, or to the unique nature of their particular systems, although the same stories are being played out in the widest variety of systems, in a full spectrum of circumstances, and with players of all personality types.

In my writings over the years I have described whole system phenomena and how our blindness to these phenomena results in personal stress, interpersonal tension and breakdown, and system disintegration. In *Power and Position* (1977)[1] I described some of the familiar stories and "system diseases" that were being played out regularly in our Power Labs: breakdowns that system members experienced as personal failings but that in fact were systemic. In *The Possibilities of Organization* (1986, 1992)[2] I described the familiar organizational story that ends with burdened Tops, oppressed Bottoms, torn Middles, and righteously screwed Customers. In *Space Work* (1992)[3] I described the familiar stories in which peers regularly fall out of partnership—Tops into turf warfare, Bottoms into groupthink, and Middles into alienation. In a series of "Middle" papers culminating with *In the Middle* (1994)[4] I described the familiar weakening of individuals and disintegration of groups occupying the middle space in systems. In *Seeing Systems* (1995)[5] I presented a framework for seeing what we system members are usually blind to: the ways in which the structure and processes of our systems as wholes shape our consciousness.

In all these writings I have demonstrated the power of "system sight"—that is, if we can see these system phenomena as they are happening, we then have the possibility of avoiding the familiar destructive consequences and creating more satisfying and constructive stories for ourselves and our systems. The challenge lies in the "if we can see these system phenomena as they are happening."

We are system creatures. Our hearts and minds are shaped by the structure and processes of the whole systems of which we are a part. Until we recognize and learn to work with that reality of our existence, we are likely to continue to do needless damage to ourselves, to others, to our systems, and to other systems. When we are blind to whole system phenomena, we are at their mercy; only when we see and understand these phenomena are we able to create sane and healthy social systems for all humankind.

Does the solitary ant comprehend the complex processes of the Hill, or the bee grasp the intricate workings of the Hive? It seems inconceivable, but who knows? What, then, do we make of ourselves? We human beings may be the most social of all creatures, given the vast array of human systems of which we are a part—families, organizations, sports teams, volunteer groups, religious institutions, schools and universities, armies, small businesses, friendship groups. Can we comprehend the workings of these systems? Can we see the wholes of which we are a part? And if we are able to see systems, what new leadership and membership possibilities does that open up for us? This is the question I continue to explore.

The development of system sight—and the possibilities such sight offers for creating sane, healthy, creative, and less destructive human systems—is a worthy challenge for us human beings and a step up the evolutionary ladder.

INTRODUCTION

◊

The Power Lab and the Search for System Leadership

The First Encounter

Things aren't getting out of control, are they, Barry? The year is 1969, the place a conference center in West Virginia. Thirty of us—staff and participants—have come together to explore the subject of institutional racism. This is to be an experiential program. Rather than discussing issues of institutional racism in the abstract, we will create a setting that will enable us to experience at least some of these issues clearly and dramatically, and then to learn from these experiences. To that end, we have divided ourselves into the Haves and Have Nots. The Have Nots have been stripped of their money, car keys, credit cards, and other personal belongings and have been assigned to rather primitive living quarters that stand in sharp contrast to the more plush accommodations of the Haves.[1]

Within minutes the Have Nots have closeted themselves behind locked doors. I'm a staff member, supposedly having access to all parts of the society, but the Have Nots have little interest in my role (I am just another one of "Them") so I am barred from their meetings. This is not fitting neatly into my paradigm of "workshop behavior."

Within hours we discover that the Have Nots are not the only ones without transportation; they have disabled all the cars at the conference center. Events move quickly, much more quickly than we staff members have been accustomed to. (In our previous workshop experience, "hot" action was civilized verbal confrontation among people who at all times remained seated around a table.) With locking doors and disabling cars we are entering a whole new arena. And this within the first hours of a ten-day program! (To be continued on page 14.)

The Society of New Hope

And so began my first encounter with what was to become the Power Lab. Much of what I know about systems and the possibilities of system power and leadership I have learned from the Power Lab.

For the past thirty years people from around the world have come to the Craigville Conference Center on Cape Cod in Massachusetts to deepen their understanding of power and powerlessness in social system life and to strengthen their skills as system members and leaders.[2]

The central feature of the Power Lab, as it has evolved over the years, is a three-class community, the Society of New Hope. There are the Elite, who own and control most of the society's resources and institutions; they own all the housing and they control the food, the bank, the court system, the newspaper, cultural activities, and employment opportunities. At the other extreme are the Immigrants, who enter the society without money or property and with little more than the clothes on their backs. And then there are the Middles, who manage the institutions of the Elite and in return are able to enjoy a modest middle-class life.

The Power Lab is not a role play in which participants break at 5 P.M. for cocktails and dinner; it is a total-immersion experience involving all aspects of people's lives—where they live, the quality of food they eat, the nature of the work they do. For example, no one has a place to sleep or food to eat unless he or she works (as manager or laborer) in the Elite's institutions, thereby earning the currency needed to rent housing, buy meals, and purchase other supplies.

I think of the Power Lab as a *magnicosm* of system life. It is a magnified microcosm in that it creates and magnifies conditions that are familiar to most (if not all) of us in our families, our organizations, and as citizens of the world: the condition of *topness,* when we have the designated responsibility for a system or part of a system and we control resources (funds, opportunities, favors, access) that others value; the condition of *bottomness,* when others control the resources we value; and the condition of *middleness,* when we are functioning between two or more individuals or groups having differing and sometimes conflicting demands of us. It is important not to confuse *position* with *condition.* One may occupy a top position in a system, yet at various times in different interactions experience topness, middleness, and bottomness. Even if one were to create a totally flat organization, the conditions of topness, middleness, and bottomness would be present.

Insider and Outsider

For participants the Power Lab has been an opportunity to come to grips with their personal issues around power and systems; for me it has been another kind of laboratory, an opportunity to observe and participate in more than forty societies from their beginning to their end. These many experiences—sometimes as participant in the society and sometimes as observer outside the society—have shaped my thinking about the whole range of human social systems, from the family to the organization, the nation, and the world. From these experiences I have begun to understand what systems are, how they function, how their structures and processes shape our consciousness as system members, and the implications of all this for system power and leadership.

I believe that my experience as sometime participant and sometime observer mirrors the insider/outsider aspects of system leadership. As insiders it is critical for us to be in touch with our feelings, to let the system wash over us, to use our experiences—anxieties, discomforts, intuitions—as clues to what is happening not just to us but to our system; to use our feelings as prompts that our system needs change and that we can change this system by changing our relationship to it. As outsiders it is useful for us to stand aside and be witness to our system, to detach ourselves from it, to see the whole of it, to understand how the processes of the whole are affecting the lives of system members and the functioning of the whole, to know what is missing and what needs to be strengthened.

Leadership Lessons

My intention is to share with you the lessons I have learned from the Power Lab for the light they can shed on your roles as system member and leader. The following lessons are topics we will explore more thoroughly throughout the book.

Power is not a dirty word. Power—though often treated as an outmoded relic of ancient times, irrelevant to our more enlightened era—is an essential element of system leadership. System power is the ability to act in ways that fundamentally transform whole systems, elevating them to new possibilities of experience and accomplishment for their members and for the systems as wholes. System leadership is quite a different order of business from system management. Management has to do with working within the accepted mission, structure, and direction of the system—smoothing things out, marshaling resources, removing roadblocks, motivating the members, streamlining processes, increasing efficiency, and so forth. By contrast, system leadership has to do with breaking the system out of its current patterns, radically transforming the system's mission, direction, traditions, and culture, elevating the system to previously unattained levels of performance. The business of management is to strengthen the system as it is; the challenge of leadership is to create what else the system can be.

System power is the ability to bring the system to self-awareness. System power moves are those that convert system blindness into system sight, such that members see the system as a whole, understand what is happening to it, recognize how it came to its current condition, have a sharpened picture of the issues it is dealing with, and see clear choices for action. Such moves "turn on the lights" for system members. It is an irony of system life that unilateral actions, which on the surface seem undemocratic, may in fact be the most democratic in that by creating system sight they allow for enlightened choice.

Position does not determine power. The leadership I am describing—that which aims for radical system transformation—is a possibility regardless of one's position in the system, and it requires the courage to wade into dangerous waters. There is a perverse comfort system members can enjoy by believing that power is not a possibility for them, that only those in power positions can make a difference. The Begging with Barry story (Part I, Chapter 4) is illuminating in this regard. In that situation, my partner and I generated fundamental system change from a position that is traditionally fractionated and powerless. Position was not the determining factor in that situation, nor is it ever. The determining factors for system power are: the *belief* that one can make a difference, a *deep understanding* of system process, and the *courage* to act.

Some leadership acts are of necessity unilateral. Consensus and group decision making are valuable processes for creating shared commitment to action; these same processes can also kill what the leader intuitively knows has to happen for the good of the system. Some readers, for example, may take offense to my stories in Part I, particularly those in which I make unilateral power moves. In Part III, Chapter 11, we will examine unilateral actions in the context of the politicization of power—the tendency to constrain one another and ultimately weaken our systems by taking what are neutral processes and politicizing them, valuing certain ones while demonizing others.

Intuition comes to the prepared mind. In Parts II and III you will be presented with some deep knowledge of systems. The power of such knowledge lies in its ability to put our feelings in context and to point the way to action alternatives. The challenge is to honor both our feelings and our minds.

Power comes from creative tension. Sometimes there is power in *not* deciding, in living with the tension between yes and no, between giving and withholding, for it is out of that tension that creative possibilities beyond yes or no, giving or withholding, can emerge. This is the lesson that came to me most clearly in "The First Encounter," Part I, Chapter 1.

Power is the management of system energy. Energy is a much under-used dimension of system life, yet it is central to the quality of life of system members and to the power of whole systems. System power is acting in ways that mobilize and focus system energy, sharpen issues that are blurred, and unfreeze the system from an unproductive status quo so that it can move on to higher levels of existence. The enemies of energy are fear, discomfort, and values. In this regard, see particularly "One That Got Away," Part I, Chapter 3.

Instead of fixing ourselves, we might do better to focus on changing the system by changing our relationship to it. Our feelings of anxiety, anger, frustration, or powerlessness are often clues to the condition of our systems. Instead of fixing or calming ourselves through therapy, drugs, or alcohol, we need to change our systems by changing our relationships to them. See "Leadership Lessons from the Inside," Part I, Chapter 5.

Real possibility often begins just at the point where we feel there is no possibility. It is at that place where we are totally stuck, where we feel that nothing else is possible, that real possibility begins. See "Begging with Barry," Part I, Chapter 4.

It is possible—desirable—to be free in the context of system life. Freedom in systems is the ability to seize the opportunity of the moment without being constrained by our role, our history, or the expectations of others. If freedom is seizing the moment, deep system knowledge lets us see the moment so that we can seize it. See "Leadership Lessons from the Inside," Part I, Chapter 5.

Systems tell stories. Systems regularly fall into archetypal stories that are limiting and destructive for the system and its members. We will examine three such stories: (1) the Top, Middle, Bottom Story (Part II, Chapter 6); (2) the Story of Righteous Warfare between Culture and Counterculture (Part IV, Chapter 14); and (3) the Story of the Dominants and the Others (Part IV, Chapters 15 and 16). System leadership is the ability to recognize these stories as they are happening, to step out of the predictable, limiting, and destructive stories and create newer, more satisfying, and more productive stories.

System leadership involves seeing systems as wholes, and working with the processes of the whole. System leadership calls for more than getting the whole system in the room; it entails seeing the whole even when it is not in the room, understanding the processes of the whole, and working with these processes to create sane and healthy human systems. In Part III we will examine three pairs of universal whole system processes: individuation and integration, differentiation and homogenization, stabilization and change. We will see how these processes contribute to system health; we will see the importance of keeping these processes in balance; and we will see how they regularly fall out of balance and the consequences of imbalance for system life. We will see how these neutral processes are politicized and the destructive consequences of such politicization. And we will explore the possibility of creating remarkable human systems by mastering these processes.

This book is divided into four parts. In Part I, I tell a few stories of my life inside New Hope and the lessons I have derived from those experiences.

In Part II, I share the lessons I have gained in my role as anthropologist to New Hope. Here we will see our first system story: the predictable lives and dilemmas of Tops, Middles, and Bottoms in system life. In "Last Hope, Lost Hope" (Chapters 7 and 8) we will see how this story plays itself out in the life of one Power Lab.

In Part III, the focus is on seeing systems as wholes. Here I introduce what I call "exhilarating concepts," frameworks that derive their excitement from their universality, from their ability to describe systems at all levels and of all types. We will focus on one set of concepts that will enable us to see, understand, and work with systems as wholes.

In Part IV, we return to the experience of life inside the system, but here the system is the all-encompassing system of the world. Each of us is one small player in that world. As members of the cosmos, our challenges are to allow the processes of the whole to wash over us and to use our deep knowledge of systems both to understand the world and to take action in it. In this section you will also find the second system story, Righteous

Warfare between Culture and Counterculture, and our third and final system story, the Terrible Dance of Power.

What ties all this together is the sense of ourselves as system creatures. We exist not in isolation but as integral components of a wide variety of whole human systems—families, organizations, communities, nations, the world. Our experiences of ourselves and others are shaped by the processes of these wholes. When we ignore our systemic nature we fall into predictable, limiting, and destructive patterns of interaction. System leadership is about transforming systems, elevating them to new levels of possibility. The key ingredients of system power are: the belief that we can make a difference to our systems, deep knowledge of the processes of the whole, and the courage to act.

I wish all of us well in our quest for enlightened system power and leadership.

Part I

Lessons from the Inside

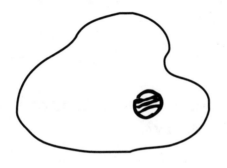

(continued from page 5.)

CHAPTER

1

The First Encounter

Guerrilla action, hostage taking, negotiations, phony constitutional conventions, confrontations, fear. Why does all this feel so exhilarating? Am I a war lover, or am I catching a glimpse of possibilities beyond war and peace?

Things Aren't Getting Out of Control, Are They, Barry?...

One of the design features for that first Power Lab was to indicate the special status of the Haves by having them all wear purple arm bands. However, the cachet of purple arm bands soon faded as the Have Nots managed to steal the supply of purple material, tear it to shreds, and hang hundreds of these pieces from trees all around the property. An unsettling sight for the Haves, especially at night when the hanging shreds cast eerie shadows.

The next morning the outside world intruded. I got a call from Nancie Coan, an administrator from the National Training Laboratories (the sponsors of this program). Nancie was looking for Pat Smith who had driven down from the central office to help with registration. "Where is Pat?" asked Nancie. Unfortunately, Pat's car was among the ones that had been disabled. I don't recall my exact reply, but I am sure it lacked the coherence Nancie expected from all of us. "Things aren't getting out of control, are they, Barry?" "Oh no," I assured her, although out of *my* control was precisely how I would have described things.

What Is Out of Bounds?

Personal lessons came quickly. For example, I felt that I needed to resolve this matter of Pat Smith in a hurry. I made my way over to the Have Nots' quarters and in my most reasonable manner explained the situation: that Pat needed to get back to work, that she was not part of our "game," and that we needed to get her car back in operation. It was as simple as that. Unfortunately for me, the Have Nots had their own logic: You want Pat's car; we want something from you. What we settled on was Pat's car in return for a car of their own. I felt that they got the better of the deal, but I was relieved that Pat had gone on her way and that, for the time being at least, Nancie Coan was held at bay.

From Fellow Traveler to Hostage

One evening the Haves were meeting; they were planning a constitutional convention. Their idea was to teach the Have Nots a lesson in institutional oppression: the convention was to be designed to give the illusion of democracy but at the end of the day would yield no substantial changes. As this conversation was going on, right outside their window the Have Nots had organized a lively demonstration. Betty Friedan, a Have, caught sight of the demonstration.[1] She rose to announce, "This (the Have meeting) is boring; that (the Have Not demonstration) is where the action is," and she promptly marched out. Her intention was to join up with the Have Nots, but once again the Have Nots had their own plans. Betty was captured, taken hostage, and held for ransom. And once again I received the message: the Have Nots had something they wanted to discuss with me.

I went to where they were holding Betty. "We want all of our belongings returned within the next twenty minutes or we're taking Betty down the road (in the car I had provided), stripping her naked, calling the major news agencies, and telling them where they can find Betty Friedan. You've got twenty minutes." I was stunned. *Is this really happening? How am I supposed to respond to this?* Betty looked at me. "Don't sweat it, Barry," she said. So we waited. The deadline passed. We heard nothing further from our hostage takers, who apparently had lost interest in us. We noticed that no one was paying attention to us, so Betty and I walked out and returned to the safety of the Haves.

Power Struggle within the Hidden Third Class

We were midway through the program when a disagreement broke out among the staff as to how to proceed. One point of view was that we should end the Have/Have Not experience, equalize the social classes, and move on to other exercises and activities dealing with institutional racism. I argued against ending the societal experience. The end-it-now proponents insisted that there were important aspects of institutional racism that wouldn't be covered if we played this societal game endlessly; a second issue was that the game was heating up figuratively and, possibly literally. We learned from the Conference Center owners that Have Nots had been around inquiring about gasoline. What was that about? Were they simply interested in tanking up their sole automobile, or did they have other plans? We had images of bonfires and burning buildings. By this time, what with the many confrontations, negotiations, hostage taking, and threats I had lived through, I was well past fear and deep into arrogance. Nothing was going to stop me; not even the threat of fire would lead me to call a halt to the exercise.

I also had a theoretical point underlying my resistance to ending the societal experience. We (the staff) were the power in this system; we were the third, "hidden" class; the Haves enjoyed the luxuries we gave and the Have Nots were living in conditions we created; we were the ones who could decide whether to return the Have Nots' goods, to end the society or continue it; and we were the ones who were now feeling the pressure (the heat) from below. The program was about institutional racism, it was about changing systems from the inside up and out, and that was precisely the point we were at; they (Haves and Have Nots) had to deal with us. I thought I was eloquent in making my case to the other staff members, but I convinced no one. In the end, the issue was resolved by a wrestling match as the fire-fearing staff member and I struggled over the keys to the storage area where the Have Nots' belongings were held. I lost both the intellectual match and the physical one; the society ended and we moved on to the other activities. The exercises and conversations we engaged in (including a male beauty contest designed by Betty Friedan) were rich and varied, and I was ready to confess that possibly I had been wrong.

The Future Has Been Canceled

On the last night of the program, participants worked in small groups developing action plans for dealing with institutional racism in their back-home systems. Jim Kunen and I moved from group to group listening to the plans.[2] There was a consistency to them: all appeared to be "downward" oriented, dealing only with those areas over which participants had direct control. For most educational programs such plans might be more than adequate, but ours was a program on institutional racism and our sights were set higher: to work at changing the very culture, structure, rules, and traditions of the systems of which we were a part. And this meant dealing *upward* in the system.

I had very little sleep that night. I felt justified in my earlier position—*They needed to deal with us*—but I had lost that battle. Was there anything to be done now? I felt that the program was falling short of its potential, and as dean of the program, I was feeling responsible for that failing. I can't account for all the inner turmoil I was experiencing—some messy mix of a need for personal redemption, competitiveness, responsibility, the chance to be the hero/savior. Whatever it was, it wouldn't let me sleep. Gradually, as the night wore on, a plan began to take shape; by the time the sun rose I knew what to do, I knew it was just the right move to make, and I was frightened half out of my wits. I also knew that I was not going to share this plan with the other staff members, convinced that if I did, they would veto it.

All of us—staff and participants—met together that last morning of the program; there was little left to do but say our goodbyes and make plans for our reunion, for built into the program was a three-day gathering some months down the road to review progress on our individual projects. However, I had other plans. I stood in front of the group, I shared my observations of their downward-oriented action plans, and then I announced that the three-day follow-up was canceled. Given the nature of these action plans, I said that I saw little purpose in our getting together. With the cancellation of the follow-up there was a good sum of money left in our budget. I told the group that I would be up in my cabin, and if people came to me with *worthwhile* projects, I would be willing to talk business. And with that I left the room. It is important to note that I had absolutely no authority to make any of these decisions; I was a contract worker for National Training Laboratories; it was not my business to cancel programs or make alternate budget decisions. Had any participant or staff member called headquarters, he or she would have been assured that I could not do what I said I was doing, and had I called headquarters asking for permission to make this move, I am quite sure they would have said no.

As you can imagine, folks were stunned. As I was leaving, I could feel the anger in the room; one staff member said, "He can't do that." I went to my cabin and waited. No one came. An hour passed; I had no thought as to what to do next. I went back to the building where the others were meeting; I stood outside and continued to wait. Finally Jim Kunen came out. He told me several things: First, that folks were very angry at me. Second, that several had come around to agree with my observation regarding their projects (which heartened me somewhat). And third, that they were stuck: I had put them in an impossible bind, first chiding them for their inability to deal upward in their systems, and now asking them to come hat in hand to me, who would judge the worthiness of their plans. "They won't come," Jim said. And I agreed.

Well, if they wouldn't come to me, then I would go to them. I developed an action plan that I thought *was* worthy of us. I asked to speak to the group and was granted permission. When I entered the room there were no friendly greetings, only stony faces. I laid out my plan; there was no reaction (no reaction was clearly part of *their* plan) and I was asked to leave the room. Twenty minutes later I was invited back in. The room was electric. My plan had been dismissed, and in its place the group members had developed a much more powerful plan involving all of us. It was clear that they had gone well beyond me, and you could feel the excitement and commitment in the room. We were going to work together to find ways to deal with institutional racism. (One of these revitalized projects succeeded in having state legislation regarding education and racism introduced and passed.)

What's in It for Me?

Once I had experienced this workshop, I was never going to let it go. Three years were to pass before we were able to create and then begin to institutionalize Power Labs. And so it has been, for close to thirty years. All of the theoretical frameworks I have developed had their beginnings in that first crude, unpolished, wild program. It was all there waiting to be elaborated: creative tension; power moves; the power of differentiation; the uniquely different worlds (or spaces) of Tops, Middles, and Bottoms; energy (mobilization, growth, unfreezing) as a value of its own; seeing systems as wholes (what IT is) and seeing the processes of the whole (what IT does).

I've always considered myself an odd person to be central to the Power Lab; in my own terminology I am "loose"—that is, soft rather than tough, inclined to say yes when in my heart I mean no, to give when I should withhold, to allow when stopping would be more appropriate.[3] Not the most fitting profile for Mr. Power Lab. So, as one might imagine, all of that tough action at the program—negotiations, hostage taking, confrontation—required great energy on my part (it was there that I saw clearly the straight-line connection between terror and bravery), and it changed me profoundly.

I flew back to Boston. I was exhausted. I was met at the airport by my wife and daughters (then 11 and 9 years old). I needed sleep, but my daughters, not having seen me for two weeks, had other plans. With great exuberance they rushed up to me. "Can we go bowling, Daddy?" Given my exhaustion, bowling stood right up there with tooth extractions on my list of preferred activities, but what came out of my mouth was neither yes nor no. "What's in it for me?" I said. The children were stunned; this was not the way it usually went with loose Daddy. I explained to them that I was exhausted, that I had had a hard week, and that I didn't really want to go bowling unless there was something really good in it for me. Their first reaction was to get all giggly and offer things like a hundred kisses. Sweet, but no good. And then, right before my eyes, without any instructions in the art of negotiation, my daughters invented the caucus. "We need to talk about this," said the older one, and off they went. They returned with some serious proposals—good but not quite good enough. We worked these around some; they went back to caucus. I was energized in this process, as were they (by now I could easily have gone bowling); we were dealing with one another in a new way. They came back with a very strong list (household chores, a commitment not to fight with each other for a week). We had a deal.

Lessons

What is happening to me here? What am I discovering that has relevance to system life and system leadership?

1. Something about power moves. Clearly there is something outrageous about my "cancellation of the future." Underhanded, dishonest, manipulative, unilateral, arrogant. All of these could be used to describe the action. Yet there is other thinking to be developed here, something about the connection between one's condition within a system (for example, my feeling weak, confused, angry, unfulfilled) and

the condition of the system itself (its underutilized potential); and there is something about the possibility of system power moves—unilateral actions that can change both of these conditions: one's life in a system as well as the life of the system itself.

2.   Something about robustness. Something about moving from acceptable to exceptional. Had I not intervened in the system, the program still would have been a success; participants would have been satisfied, their projects might have been productive, and no one would have had a sense of something missing. Yet the system was elevated to a whole new level of energy, creativity, and productivity, one that none of us could have anticipated. Isn't system leadership about making possible these quantum leaps?

3.   The power of creative tension—not saying yes when I feel like saying no and not saying no when that doesn't feel right either, neither yes nor no, neither giving nor withholding, just living in the tension between and allowing creative possibilities to emerge. Here are the seeds of my theory of interaction comfort.[3] When we are uncomfortable with the interaction and its tension, we go loose or tight, both of which cut off the possibilities of creation. System leaders are creators; they need to be able to live in that tension between giving and withholding, between allowing and denying, between yes and no.

4.   What else am I discovering? The power of the Power Lab, its potential as a learning environment for others…and for me. I'll never let it go.

2

You Bet a Bus, I'll Raise You an Airplane

A school bus magically appears. Leaflets drop from the sky. My room is stripped bare. The unified society (communists) and the free society (capitalists) clash. Such energy! Energy is a dimension that does not enter much into our political debate, yet it is central to the development of healthy, sane societies.

War or Peace; Alive or Dead

Over the years there has been a shift in the tone of the Power Lab from more confrontational (tough) stances at both the top and bottom to more collaborative ones. (I am describing a general shift; there have been several exceptions to this rule in both the early and latter days.) Although the tone has changed, the underlying systemic tensions have remained constant. At the top: Do we hold on to the power or share it? Do we maintain the traditions or change them? At the bottom: Do we work within the system or rebel against it? Do we use soft or hard tactics to change it? In the 1970s, Power Labs were for the most part more eruptive than they became in the mid-'80s and into the '90s. (Is it possible that in periods of cultural turmoil, system members are more willing to risk the uncertainties associated with power moves; whereas in times of relative stability, there is more reluctance to rock the boat?) In the early days, the Elite were more willing to maintain their difference (their Eliteness) and to play with the power of their positions; there were sharper confrontations, rebellions, break-ins (in a number of programs people broke the same pane of glass to gain entry to the Elite house; we considered replacing that pane with one on a hinge with a sign reading "In case of forced entry, push here"); there were attempted takeovers of the dining room. Action, reaction, and polarization. People in different camps would meet in airports years later, and the old tensions would come right back. One can look at these interactions and ask: Is this the kind of behavior you want to encourage in people? Competitive, confrontational, destructive...and yet very much alive, energizing, creative.

The latter-day Labs tend to be marked by a greater mix of "enlightenment" and caution. This is often translated into a desire to avoid those "destructive" system forms of the past and to create the new worlds of collaboration, partnership, transformation, and so forth. Much more civilized, collaborative, non-confrontational...and, to me at least, much more boring.

The more energized experiences offered a glimpse into one of the major sources of intractability in prison uprisings or guerrilla war: if peace promises nothing more than the return to numbing routine or grinding poverty, then organized rebellion can be an attractive alternative, a more interesting and enlivening game to play, *even if there is little hope of winning.*[1]

The questions arise: Do we get stuck on the polarities of peace versus war, giving versus withholding, tight versus loose, liberal versus conservative? Who could argue against peace if war were the only alternative? Must peace be so boring and war so destructive? I think of Ryan Malan escaping from the warfare, fear, and terror of life in South Africa and finding peace in the United States, only to find himself bored by that peaceful life and missing the excitement and challenge of life in South Africa.[2]

The Fear of Energy

There is reason to avoid energy if its predictable outcomes are riots, escalating conflicts, wars, and destructive competition. But energy is more complex than that; it is also connected with aliveness, vibrancy, and growth both for ourselves and our systems.

And just as there is danger in unleashing uncontrolled energy, so are there costs in avoiding it. *Don't do that, it will only upset them.* Well, it won't *only* upset them; it might also bring them to life, mobilize their thinking, cause them to stretch and grow; and their reactions just might do the same for us. The unrelenting avoidance of energy has the predictable costs of deadening us and them. Sometimes the greatest service we can be to one another is to be the wall that others must deal with.

Energy is a dimension that does not enter much into our political debate, yet it is central to the development of healthy societies. Those high-energy Power Labs were so beautiful to behold—people putting themselves at risk, venturing into new challenges, testing, stretching, growing; their faces would change, and even their posture. The desire for that kind of energy without destructive warfare is what lies behind the search for robust systems.

The following is a story from a Power Lab in the mid-1970s. The Elite were meeting. The very location of their meeting said a good deal about them as players. As Elite they could live wherever they chose. Most Elite selected the big house overlooking the ocean, far removed from the "downtown" housing of the Immigrants and Middles. These Elite, however, wanted to be in the middle of the action, so they chose housing that was centrally located but of poor quality—tiny rooms, unheated, but in the action.

As they were meeting, an Immigrant came to the door, poked his head in, and asked: "Does anyone want a ride?" Now, how was this possible? Immigrants had no cars and no money. The Elite looked out the window and saw that the Immigrant had driven up in a yellow school bus! (Later we discovered that this participant had come to the program a day early to scope out the territory. Who does that now? Today's participants are more civilized; they come when they are told to come.) He chatted up a woman on the property who happened to be a school bus driver, and at an opportune moment she let him use the bus. The Elite were impressed...and felt a surge of competition

In their meeting the Elite had been discussing what to do about a problem they were facing. They had constructed their system as an educational institution; they were the Deans, their Middles were the instructors, and the Immigrants were the students. The problem was, *no one was going to class!* The school bus incident inspired Chuck Colbert (a fictitious name), a member of the Elite, who happened to be a pilot and who also happened to have parked his plane at a nearby airport. The Elite printed hundreds of fliers—*Get your ass back to class!*—they piled into Chuck's plane, buzzed the lab site, and dropped their leaflets. While the leaflets were drifting down from the sky, the Immigrants were on a rampage—breaking into houses, stealing food from the kitchen, and completely stripping Karen's and my apartment (we had been identified as Resource Persons to the Elite) down to the light bulbs and toilet paper. The sole witness to the Elite fly-by was Karen, standing in the center of the village, watching the plane diving low and dropping its leaflets...which the wind immediately carried off, out of sight, to a nearby pond. So much for dramatic gestures.

The Power of One

It was in these sharply confrontational encounters that one could see the emergence of distinct cultures within the society, and the politicization of these cultures. The Immigrants were the Unified Society, the Elite were the champions of the Free Society, and the Middles were generally split, some for the Free and some for the Unified. The Immigrants found their strength in their unity; there was much sharing of resources (to each according to his or her need), joint decision making, and a strong sense of camaraderie; along with this unity came powerful pressures for uniformity and conformity. There were long and draining arguments over which strategy to pursue (hard or soft) in their dealings with the Elite. At times there were extreme codes of behavior to be adhered to in order to be an accepted member of this "new world"—elaborate initiation rights that sometimes included loyalty oaths and self-revelatory confessions. The Elite, on the other hand, were the champions of the Free Society, often mocking the Immigrants as the mindless herd. To the Immigrants the Elite were the fascists, and to the Elite the Immigrants were the socialists or communists.

After my room had been stripped bare (my most precious object, my notebook, included in the loot), I had my own experience of the Free versus Unified Societies. Stripped, I felt completely free. I remember now so clearly, twenty-five years later, strolling down the street, passing those who had just colluded in stripping me of my belongings and singing, "Freedom's just another word for nothing left to lose." Gone were my Elite responsibilities. Beholden to no one but myself. I could do whatever I wanted, and my freedom stood in sharp contrast to the uniformity and conformity of the Immigrants. I tormented them with freedom. They went off as a group to play volleyball; I tagged along *(Can I play?)*; since their code required excluding me, and since I insisted on playing, there could be no volleyball game. Wow, what power! I'd disrupt their meetings, I'd offer to wash dishes after their meal of food stolen from the dining room. I had some cash, and my car, surprisingly, was still operable; I purchased hot dogs and set up a hot dog stand directly in front of their house.

At one point, I offered one of the Immigrants a trip to Provincetown, just him, a young graduate student, and me, master of the Power Lab. "Screw all this, let's just head off and have a good time; and if it will make you feel better, we can even talk theory." I saw the look in his eyes, the lure of freedom, but no, he just couldn't do it. I am sure that to the Immigrants (and possibly to the reader) I looked like a wild man, a lunatic; but I felt totally free, restrained by no one and nothing, and to me the Immigrants looked like the lumbering herd, each member captive to the group.

Lessons

What is happening to me here?

◊

1. I am intrigued with human energy; I see the beauty in people as they stretch beyond their usual day-to-day limitations. They seem more fully alive as they put themselves at risk, as they step into the unknown, as they face their fears and move through them rather than being controlled by them. At the same time, I am aware of the dangers of energy—the violence, destruction, and warfare that come with it. Instead of war versus peace, why aren't we talking about system leadership as the management of human energy?

2. Related to this is the question of whether peace suppresses the potential of systems. If conditions are OK, why risk the uncertainties of energizing? The '60s and '70s were periods of pain and divisiveness in the United States—the Vietnam War, President Nixon and Watergate, the civil rights movement, the oil crisis and its dampening effects on the economy. Was it that pain and dissatisfaction that opened people to search for better ways; to question the status quo; to rebel, test, experiment in the Power Lab as well as in society at large? By contrast, in times of peace and prosperity, the prevailing mood—in New Hope and in society—is to conserve, to keep things running smoothly, to not jeopardize what you have. The cost? The self-inflicted suppression of energizing that could elevate the system to a more robust level of existence.

3. I am intrigued by the systemic nature of system form, such as that of the Free Society and the Unified Society. How easy it is to make a case for either of these—the virtues of each, and the limitations. I see how easy it is to justify either form while demonizing the other. Did Karl Marx create communism? Not likely; isn't it more probable that social class differences—the poverty and powerlessness of the lower

classes and the abuses of power by the upper classes—created Karl Marx? We will return to this matter in Part III, where we examine whole system processes and how neutral processes are often politicized to the detriment of systems and their members. What would system leadership look like if one saw system processes clearly, freed of the need to politicize them, freed of the need to extol the virtues of one and demonize the other?

4.   I come away from the Power Lab seeing the world differently. I am seeing the whole and the connections among the parts. I drive to Boston from Cape Cod, seeing the huge homes and spacious grounds in largely white and wealthy Osterville, and the largely black, poor, and crowded tenements of Roxbury, and I see clearly how the two are connected and part of the whole. I awake one night from a dream about the Power Lab; I sit straight up in bed and say to no one in particular, "It's alive." I see the New Hope Society—and all systems—not as collections of individuals and not as sets of random events, but as entities with their own forms and functions. I begin to see and wonder about ITs properties, and about the role of leadership in working with those properties.

One That Got Away

My plan is to accuse four blacks and one white of being derelict in their duties, and eventually to evict them from their house. This is an outrageous move—potentially racist, clearly unilateral, and coming out of the blue. I encourage you to see it that way, and then try to see it another way.

There Is No Middle

It begins the usual way. I awake at 3 A.M. anxious, worried; something about the Lab is troubling me. *There is no Middle in this society.* There are five people living in the Middle house; they sit together at the Middle table in the dining room, they eat their Middle meals. The problem is they don't pay for their meals, they pay no rent for their house, and they serve no societal Middle functions. These Middles have become like the proverbial elephant in the room—everyone sees it, yet everyone acts as if it's not there. There is no Middle in this society, and I am feeling responsible, at least in part. Here is the background.

The time is the mid-'80s. We were experimenting with a design variation. Each staff member was to be coach to a particular part of the system; I was coach to the Elite, and my colleague Joe Meier was coach to the Middles. The Elite had arrived a day early; part of their work was preparing for the arrival of the Middles: evaluating them, assigning them to the various traditional Middle roles, and then working with them to prepare for the arrival of the Immigrants. A plan was developed for this initial meeting: determining which Elite would handle which part of the orientation, establishing a flow of events and a timetable. The Elite planned to interview each Middle separately, then caucus to make their decisions, and finally assign the Middles their societal roles. The Elite were ready. But then reality hit, and we were all in for a surprise.

Four of the five soon-to-be Middles were African Americans (and the four came to describe the fifth as "as good as black"). It was a fluke; never before had we had that many African Americans clustered in one part of the system. It was also a rare experience for our soon-to-be Middles. There was instant bonding. That, coupled with some skillful coaching by Joe, led to an off-and-running powerhouse Middle team. These Middles were not coming hat in hand to be sized up and slotted by the Elite; they had quickly formed themselves into an independent consulting firm ready to offer its services for a fee to the Elite.

When the Middles/Consulting Firm walked into the Elite office, the Elite had no idea what they were dealing with. They proceeded with the first part of their plan, which consisted of a warm welcome, introductions, providing the new arrivals with lunch, and (what was soon to prove a sore point) giving them the key to their cottage *before they signed on as Middles*. Niceties completed, it quickly became clear that this was a different breed of Middle; they were not interested in being interviewed and assigned jobs; they were here as a consulting firm. The Elite were stunned; this was not in their plan. The conversation went back and forth between "our plan" and "your plan"; it became progressively more heated, and ended with the Elite refusing to accept the new arrivals as a consulting firm and the new arrivals refusing to accept their role as Middles. The Middles/Consulting Firm left the Elite office with their key and moved into the Middle house.

And that is how life proceeded. The Elite attempted to manage the society without the Middles; the Consulting Firm went about living in their cottage, enjoying their relationships with one another, and doing whatever they chose to do. They were not working for the Elite; yet they were living in Elite property while paying no rent; they were eating in the Elite dining room without paying for meals.

That is the picture I awoke with at 3 A.M. I had been coach to the Elite and now felt that I had been doing a poor job. The Elite had made a few feeble efforts to bring the Middles into line. The Elite refused to threaten eviction, concerned that they would be unable to carry it off (which was probably accurate, yet insufficient reason for not posting eviction notices). My initial concern was with the Middles, who were probably having a pleasant enough time but not having the unique experience of living in the Middle space. Their initial fighting free of the Elite was probably a satisfying and potentially productive experience for them, yet I felt that that victory had come too easily. The Middles/Consulting Firm were the elephant in the room, and what is more, they were the African American elephant in the room. All the more reason not to see them.

Then IT hit me: the beginning of the power move. (Although I suggest that the beginning of the power move was the anxiety that woke me—the same anxiety we often choose to suppress or narcotize ourselves against.) And when I visualized the move, I really became anxious. It was outrageous. (Another promising sign.) *I would go to the Elite and volunteer to be their Middle.* I would offer to take on responsibility for managing the various neglected Middle functions. I would be a hard-working, conscientious Middle. In return I would ask for Middle pay, I would move into the Middle house, eat at the Middle table; and since I would be the only "legal" Middle in the house, I would attempt to either bring the others into line or evict them.

Why?

To suddenly step out of the sideline coach role and pop right into the middle of the action was to be a paradigm-shattering move, both for me and for others. In my previous lab experiences I had never done such a thing. This was going to set everyone's head spinning. But why do it? Undoubtedly some piece of this was personal: to reestablish my own competence, to use my knowledge, to move from frustrated powerlessness to the potential (no guarantee) of power. Was it an anti-black move? Was my motive to punish them? Was it to show up the Elite, to demonstrate that one could deal with the elephant in the room?

To truly understand the move, one needs to get inside my framework for systems change. When we are in the potential power situation, three common factors influence our choices: safety, values, and interaction comfort.

Safety. With regard to safety, we assess the move in terms of its potential for endangering us. Safe moves are attractive; dangerous ones are to be avoided. Wisdom lies in staying out of trouble. For many of us, safety is the first and often the only consideration. If that is the sole lens through which we look, then moves such as I was planning could never even enter our consciousness. And if the possibility of such a move were brought to our attention, it would quickly be dismissed as insanely self-destructive. Why would anyone want to do such a thing? Clearly, safety was not my primary consideration. This was not a safe move, and yet, on the basis of other considerations, it felt like just the right action to take.

Values. In terms of values, we assess potential power moves against their consonance or dissonance with our values. For example, my move involved having the Elite simply announce the change as I moved into the Middle house. There was to be no discussion or negotiation with the Middles. This was to be a fait accompli. From certain value perspectives such an action was unthinkable. From a liberal perspective it was mean-spirited, anti-black, unilateral (as opposed to consensually arrived at). From a conservative perspective one might appreciate its "anti-welfare" nature as well as its effort to respect and restore the traditional societal structure (the three-tier system, the way things ought to be); yet this move was to violate a fundamental staff/participant agreement upon which the Power Lab was built—if staff could suddenly become players, was there any stability one could count on? I am both liberal and conservative; I believe in kindness and lending a helping hand, and I believe in independence; I am attracted to the new and experimental, and I have a deep respect for tradition. But my move had little to do with liberalism or conservatism. Neither kindness nor the "restoration of the empire" entered into my considerations.

Interaction Comfort. We sometimes confuse values (liberal versus conservative) with interaction comfort (loose versus tight). As Looses we appear to be liberal, but our liberalism proceeds not from belief but from discomfort: we say yes because we're uncomfortable saying no; we give when we'd prefer to withhold but are uncomfortable doing so; we allow things to happen because we are uncomfortable stopping them. And, conversely, as Tights we are uncomfortable in giving, allowing, and saying yes. Both Loose and Tight proceed not out of belief systems but out of a lack of confidence in our ability to manage or survive in a give-and-take, open-ended interaction. I recognize my own interaction discomfort and my tendencies to go loose or tight; yet clearly this move was not the preferred mode of action for either a Loose or a Tight. I was setting myself up for maximum ambiguity; I had a clear sense of how this move would begin, but it was no sure thing that I would manage or even survive in the interaction to follow. Interaction comfort was not my driving motivation, yet the move still seemed just right.

Energy: Mobilization, Growth, Unfreezing

I propose that this trio of culprits—safety, values (liberal or conservative), and interaction comfort (looseness or tightness)—blinds us to many productive possibilities for ourselves and our systems. My move emerged from another framework, one that has to do with managing system energy.

The move would mobilize everyone. It would wake us up, get our juices flowing, increase our aliveness. It would focus otherwise diffuse energy and bring it to bear around this issue. It would get our brains working—thinking, planning, strategizing. This is not to say that mobilizing energy is always the right action to take; sometimes, such as during intense, destructive conflict and warfare, one might well choose to diffuse energy. The point is, energy—whether to mobilize or demobilize—is a dimension one would do well to attend to.

It would differentiate the system. System members at all levels would no longer be able to ignore the elephant in the room. *(Here's the elephant. Now what do we do about it?)* Differences that had been submerged would now surface. For example, I foresaw differences emerging within the Immigrant group: some folks supporting my position, some opposing it. I foresaw differences developing within the Middle group itself—differences among Middles and ambivalence *within* Middles ("Is he right?" "Are we illegal?") Differentiation sheds light on an issue: we see it from many angles, and it challenges us. *(How can we resolve our differences?)* Differentiation creates the possibility of growth. Again, this is not to imply that differentiation is always the goal to pursue. Sometimes—when, for example, we seem unable or unwilling to resolve our differences, when our differences are explosive and destructive—de-differentiation or homogenization (reducing differences and searching for commonality) is the direction in which to move. In this case, the plan struck me as just right because it would differentiate the system and challenge us to deal with our differences...and grow. But there would be the risk that it would polarize us beyond the pale of dialogue.

And finally, the move would unfreeze the current system form, thus enabling the system to move to a new level of form and function. The action would negate the current system (business as usual would no longer be a possibility); something new would have to develop in its place. Once again, unfreezing is not the universal panacea; sometimes our system is too fluid, formless, changing, and what we need to do is freeze it. In this case, however, unfreezing seemed just the right way to go.

In the early moments, when the move was forming in my mind, my reaction was more emotional than conceptual. *My* juices were flowing; I was both anxious and excited; the move *felt* just right. Only gradually did I begin to see *why* it was just right.

The De-energizing Bias

In the section above I may have diluted my case for the virtues of energizing by being overly generous, by giving equal weight to either end of the energy dimensions—mobilize or demobilize, differentiate or homogenize, unfreeze or freeze—as if each of us moves with equal ease in either direction, and as if our organizational cultures are equally supportive of either direction. Neither of these is the general rule. Energizing as described here is not something that shows up regularly in organizational vision statements; energizing moves tend to be seen as disruptive, divisive, trouble making, showboating, de-stabilizing, and so forth.

On the personal side, our habitual dimensions of choice—safety, values, and interaction comfort—have the same effect of leading us away from energizing actions. So, for example, if I am in the grip of a safety orientation—*Stay out of danger*—I might be willing to acknowledge the general value of the energizing principle while finding all sorts of reasons for avoiding the energizing action—*The time isn't right; this isn't the right move; you need to choose your battles.* The same is likely to be true if we are in the grip of our values or interaction discomfort. My point is this: most of us have little need for exercising our safety, values, or interaction discomfort muscles; they are our default responses. It is our energizing muscle that needs work.

Consensus Strikes

I wish I had a more exciting finish to this tale. Unfortunately, the end was illuminating but hardly energizing. I went to the Elite house shortly after the crack of dawn; I needed time for us to talk this through thoroughly, and if at all possible I wanted to make the move before breakfast. We met in the Elite's living room. We talked some about their feelings about how things were going (not very well, they agreed), then we discussed my diagnosis of the situation (the lack of a Middle in the society, the elephant in the room), then I made my proposal *(I will be your Middle, I will perform all Middle functions, I will live in the Middle house, I will attempt to either evict or bring the other Middles into the society; and in return all I want is Middle pay and Elite support).* As you can imagine, the Elite were initially stunned; despite my urging, they chose not to decide right away but assured me they would get back to me during or after (memory fails) breakfast. I left hopeful, charged up...and more than a little anxious. I went back to my room and gathered up what few belongings I would need.

As I walked back toward the dining room, I saw a crowd on the green, and there addressing it were the Elite. My heart sank as I heard them speak. "We need Middles," said one. "Are there any volunteers?" said another. There were no volunteers: the Immigrants were bonded and none of them was likely to step out of the pack; the existing "Middles" saw no need for more Middles, since they themselves were already in place. The Elite had talked this over; they thought a participative mode would be more satisfactory than a unilateral move, and they thought offering this up to "legitimate" members of society would be more palatable (less outrageous) than transforming a staff member into a Middle. It all made sense from their perspective; unfortunately, it made no sense at all as a power move. It was one more embarrassing moment for the Elite—lots of questions and wisecracks were directed at them, and the crowd drifted off to the dining room. There would be no Middles. Consensus, participation, reasonableness, and safety struck again.

What strikes me now as I tell this tale is my own silence when the question was asked: "Are there any volunteers?" There I was, waiting in the wings, satchel in hand. Why didn't I step forward and say, "Here I am, I'm your man, your new Middle"? Quite frankly, it's only now that that thought even enters my mind. Remarkable. I must have been in the grip of my own safety/values/interaction comfort demons. (*Too frightening a move to make; too outrageous.*) It never even entered my mind.

Lessons

What am I seeing?

◊

1.   I am thinking about "outrageous" moves and speculating that these have always been at the heart of system leadership. I picture Anwar Sadat in Cairo, Abraham Lincoln in Washington, Yitzhak Rabin in Jerusalem, waking in the night; they are anxious, something is not going well and they are feeling responsible. Then the thought floats up to consciousness. "I will go to Jerusalem," says Sadat. "That will break the logjam and begin the process of making peace with Israel." The thought comes with great clarity; he recognizes it as just the right move to make, and it frightens him. "I will issue a proclamation freeing the slaves," says Lincoln. "It will give us the high moral ground, bring all the blacks around to our cause, and make it difficult for England to support the South." "I will meet with my hated enemy Arafat and begin a peace process with the Palestinians," says Rabin. The thought comes with great clarity; he recognizes it as just the right move to make, and it frightens him. Sadat and Lincoln and Rabin made moves that shook their worlds…and all three were assassinated. Which captures much of the essence of the system power move.

2.   I am concocting a witches brew for the power move. The necessary ingredients:

- The ability to see the system as a whole—what is ITs condition, what does IT need?

- Seeing one's centrality to the system, the belief that you could make a difference.

- Experiencing one's responsibility for the system, not only that you could make a difference but that you should.

- Treating anxiety not as something to be narcotized but as a potentially productive clue that something is wrong with the system and your relationship to it.

Conversely, if you want to sleep well at night, the formula is quite simple: see yourself as a sideline player in life and believe that others, not you, are responsible for your systems.

The concept of power move will always be controversial as a legitimate aspect of system leadership, and it is unwise for the leader to ask permission or expect appreciation. Few of us enjoy being acted on; there is something distasteful about unilateral actions *(What happened to democracy, one person/one vote, consensus?)*. There are legitimate arguments to be made for involvement, participation, and consensus; yet there are other situations in which involvement, participation, and the need for consensus will guarantee that nothing productive will happen. I wish I had been able to make my move happen; there would have been quite a different story to tell. Yet, in another sense, I am delighted by the failure of the move; it reveals so much. The Elite wanted to change the plan from a unilateral power move to a participative decision making process, and so it fizzled. I thought my plan was outrageous, yet when the last hope of the plan was right in front of me, the logical power move—"Here I am; I'm your Middle"—was so outrageous it never even entered my consciousness.

Begging with Barry

I am aware that Power Lab stories may offend one's sensibilities: break-ins, stealing, confrontations, rebellions, class distinctions, unilateral power moves. And now, begging. I suppose the basic principle is: in New Hope, as in all societies, people work with what they have. Keep in mind how many millions of us each day sit in traffic jams or squeeze ourselves into crowded trains, buses, or subways, inhale poisonous fumes, spend all day in our offices (despite the beautiful weather outside), only to get back into those traffic jams, trains, or buses as we head home. Can you imagine how bizarre that might look to someone from another culture. Why would sane people do such things? You may see begging as an offensive act; if so, try also to see it as the kind of "out of the box" leadership action we need to transform our societies. When you change a system, you alter the current story; when you transform a system, you create a new story. When you see systems, transformation becomes a real possibility.

The following is a story from the 1990s.

My Goal is to Survive with My Self-Respect Intact

Enrollment was low. The only way the Lab was to happen would be if some of the staff entered the society as players. After years of writing and talking about power and powerlessness in the middle (along with specific strategies for success), I volunteered to enter the program as a Middle. Middle has always been seen as the weakest part of the New Hope Society (as well as other organizations you may be more familiar with)—torn between above and below; always harried; trying to please everyone and often pleasing no one; feeling weak, incompetent, alienated from one another. (For the full Middle syndrome, see *In the Middle*.[1]) I did not experience myself as being nervous at registration, but apparently I was: I fell and scratched myself walking in the woods; I tripped entering the registration room, and dropped and broke my precious pocket watch; and to my colleagues I looked more than a bit disoriented. As I mentioned earlier, although I write about power I do not consider myself to be a particularly powerful person; I was not entering this Middle world feeling *I'll show them how this is really done*. On the contrary, I was feeling most vulnerable: *People will know who I am; they will both be suspicious of me and expect great things from me.* My goal was to survive with my self-respect intact.

Knowing what I knew about middleness, I entered the society with a few basic resolves. One: be top when you can; that is, don't go looking to the Elite for direction or permission; decide what you think has to happen, do it, and take the consequences of your actions. Two: don't feel that you have to resolve every issue that comes your way (or dance to every tune as it's called and when it's called); that is, coach others to do for themselves what they are asking you to do, bring together contending parties to solve their own issues; basically, stay out of the middle. And three: stay connected with your Middle peers, and keep us connected with one another.

As the societal experience unfolded, these simple strategies shored me up. I could see how without them this Middle position would be maddening. Still, even armed with my strategies, the

Middle position was taking its toll. My Middle peers remained suspicious of me, partly wondering why I was in the program, but more than that, it was my interest in them that puzzled them. Why did I care about their problems? Why was I so interested in helping them? They tolerated me but watched me with wary eyes.

Then things got truly hectic. The Elite were also short-handed; one of their members-to-be never arrived at the program. On the second day of the society they recruited one of our Middles to be an assistant Elite, which left two of us to perform functions normally carried out by four or five Middles. For example, in this new downsized operation, I was responsible for meals (taking orders twice a day, getting these into the kitchen on a tight schedule, handling food complaints, supervising waiters) and for housing (collecting rents daily, seeing that housing was maintained in good order); and I managed the pub and was police chief and court officer, not to mention the complex paperwork my Elite boss had contrived in order to keep tight control over my actions. I was wearing down, as was my Middle partner, who was in constant conflict with her Elite boss (never quite doing enough).

It's the little things that matter—straws that break camels' backs. One night at dinner my partner and I were fairly worn out and depressed, when from across the room I heard an Immigrant shouting out, "Barry, these rolls are hard." *What, now the rolls are my problem?* That was it. I looked to my partner. "What do you say we quit?" It was as if a great load had lifted from her shoulders. "Let's do it." We went back to our cottage and drew up a sign, which read:

MIDDLE RETIREMENT HOME:

All visitors welcome

---

and posted it on our door. No more worries about rolls, meal tickets, citations and subpoenas. We took a walk along the beach and talked about life outside of New Hope. What freedom!

There was an illusion to all this. One did not simply retire in New Hope. This may have been our created reality, but the Elite had their own. They owned the house we were living in; they hired us to perform various functions in return for which services they paid us, which enabled us to pay the rent on this house. Our retirement home was not in their plans. They might very well have locked us out. As a precaution we removed the lock to the front door.

It has always amazed me how swiftly life moves in New Hope. Retirement had felt marvelous, but within hours it was time to move on. I spent much of the night tossing and turning. What's next? I didn't want to spend the rest of my existence in retirement, and I was concerned about what action the Elite might take next. Some time before dawn an idea began to form. Sanctuary! I became excited as the idea took shape. My partner and I would turn this house into a sanctuary, a place where members of the society, from any level, could come for relief, emergency shelter, and food. I met with my partner; she, too, had been thinking about new directions, organizing educational events and entertainment. Perfect. Sanctuary: a place for food, clothing, shelter, entertainment, and education. We argued some about the name; my partner was set against "Sanctuary." Too much of a religious connotation, which was just why I considered it perfect. I was still concerned about eviction by the Elite and thought the religious association would give them pause. Toss out a church? In the end I relented, and we came up with another name: Oasis. Down came our retirement-home sign and up went our new one.

OASIS

FREE

Food • Clothing • Shelter • Respite
• Recreation • Education •

All are welcome

We were delighted with our concept; now the only problem was how to make this happen. We had our house, temporarily at least. That took care of shelter and respite. We had more personal clothing than the Immigrants, so we could put out our own extra pieces and we could solicit donations from the Elite. So clothing was taken care of. My partner was going to search out volunteer teachers and entertainers from among the Immigrants. Our remaining problem was food. We had no food, we had no money to buy food, and the Elite controlled the dining room. How to get food? Then a thought came to me. A discomforting thought. We could go begging. Our conference center was surrounded by suburban residential areas; we could walk off the property, go door to door, and beg for food. This was not something I was particularly comfortable doing. (By now are you beginning to see these as the signs of a promising power move: an outrageous act that goes beyond current acceptable boundaries yet seems just right, and that makes you very anxious?) I met with a group of Immigrants, explained the situation to them, and asked for volunteers. Several stepped forward, and off we went with empty trash bags in search of food: the Begging with Barry Brigade.

We knocked on several doors with no success. Some folks simply said no; some seemed afraid of us; some elderly folks were very apologetic, explaining that they had barely enough food for themselves. And then the first can hit the bag. I doubt if I have had a more exhilarating moment in my life. We persisted and our bags began to fill. We returned to our house and cooked up lunch.

Before going on, I need to describe what a Middle house usually looks like in New Hope. Generally it is a barren, unexciting place. It is quiet; if Middles are there, they are usually off by themselves organizing their paperwork for their particular areas of responsibility. There is very little action, still less interaction, no smells of food, no visitors dropping in just to chat…and no fun. Absolutely no fun.

Oasis was quite another story. It became the center of community life. The aromas of food cooking on the stove filled the house; people ate, they took some of the warm clothing we had put out, they came in just to chat; they participated in several seminars that Immigrants offered; we had dancing lessons. Food, clothing, shelter, respite, education, and entertainment. Oasis was the hottest spot in town, a triumph for us Middles. Innovation, contribution, entrepreneurship, and partnership. Not the way it usually goes in the middle.

Epilogue

The day after the program, I was relaxing reading Paolo Freire's *Pedagogy of the Oppressed*.[2] There was a footnote quote from the work of Professor Alvaro Vieira Pinto. It struck me with such clarity that I gasped. In that moment I saw a whole new dimension to the Begging with Barry escapade.

After our hot lunch at Oasis I had set out with a new group of volunteer beggars, this time to another, wealthier part of town. We were much less successful, in fact we were total failures. Not a single can did we collect, not a slice of day-old bread. What we did get was the police. People in this neighborhood were nastier to us, more suspicious, and, evidently, more closely connected to the police. The patrol car pulled up, blue lights flashing. There were two officers. "There have been complaints; what you are doing is against the law unless you have a permit." (It would take ten to fourteen days to get a permit.) The message was clear: *Stop*. They drove off. What would we do now? We needed more food for supper. We decided to take our chances and resume begging. Within minutes the flashing blue lights were back. This time the message was firm: *If we catch you bothering people again, we're locking you up.* We had hit the wall; begging was over. (We did collect more food from a local church, but we considered this cheating since we agreed to replace the food following our program.)

Now here I was, the day after the program, reading this footnote:

> For Vieira Pinto, the "limit-situations" are not "the impassable boundaries where possibilities end, but the real boundaries where all possibilities begin"; they are

not "the frontier which separates being from nothingness, but the frontier which separates being from being more." (Freire, page 71.)

I slapped my head. It struck me with great clarity that the second coming of the police was *my* limit situation. I experienced the prospect of arrest as an "impassable boundary where possibility ends" and as "a frontier which separates being from nothingness." Begging was over. There was no choice. Or so it seemed.

In reading Freire it became clear that there was choice. The begging brigade (or I alone) could have stepped through that limit situation; we could have continued begging and allowed ourselves to be arrested and jailed. In doing so, that limit situation would have become a "frontier where all possibilities begin" and a place which "separated our being from being more." Let me explain.

Begging had been a personal experience for each of us; it was putting us, albeit in a limited way, in touch with some aspects of hunger and homelessness and the humiliation and rejection of begging. We also had feelings about how we had been received in this "rich part of town"—the fear, the barricade mentality, the insensitivity, the readiness to resort to police power. But all of this had been our own personal learning.

Stepping through the limit situation and allowing ourselves to be arrested and jailed would have provided us with a broader platform from which to raise issues of poverty, hunger, suburban isolation, and so forth. The local papers would welcome the story, and that story might easily have spread to other news media, local television, and possibly to national television and news services. The threat of arrest was the beginning of possibility, not the end.

Lessons

What am I seeing?

◊

1.   This story stands as proof of the incredible difference a little knowledge about systems can make. We Middles had transformed that middle space; never before and never since has the Middle space been such a vibrant center of society. We were not the usual weak, fractionated Middles; we were strong and respected members of the community. Our house was not the usual barren, soulless middle bed-room community. It became a space of creativity, contribution, and accomplishment; it was a place in which my Middle partner and I created and sustained a supportive partnership with one another; the house we created was the liveliest house in the community. My knowledge gave me strength, and leverage. I understood what the middle space could do to people individually and collectively; I knew not to take things personally; I knew to put extra effort into staying in relationship with my associate Middles; I knew that I didn't have to dance to every tune that was called as it was called; I knew that rather than doing for others I could coach people to do for them-selves. All of this kept me from being personally torn apart in the middle, and it kept us Middles from being torn from one another. This is not to say that all of this came easily. We still experienced all the pressures of that middle space, but we had the knowledge and skills to manage them. There is an old Arabic saying: Take what you want, says the Lord, only pay for it. There were risks we had to take: to step out of the middle as it had been defined for us, and to find our own independent way of being in the middle.

2.   I am seeing how the possibility of system leadership is not limited to Tops, that creative transformation can come from any part of the system. Once again the lesson is clear: position is not the determining

factor; courage, the willingness to take risks, and a deep understanding of systems are.

3. I am seeing that as you pass through one limit situation there is another waiting for you, and that just as you think you have reached the limits of your being, there are possibilities of being waiting to be entertained.

CHAPTER

5

Leadership Lessons from the Inside

I've learned many things from my experiences in New Hope: lessons for the heart and lessons for the head. Lessons for the heart have taught me about the possibilities of freedom within the context of system life, and lessons for the head have provided me with powerful knowledge about the nature of systems. Lessons for the heart and the head together provide the basis for enlightened system leadership and membership.

Lessons for the Heart: Freedom

We humans are system creatures; we are components of families, communities, organizations, churches, nations, bowling leagues, volunteer groups, neighborhoods, and on and on. In this systemic existence of ours we are never wholly independent; we interact with others, influencing them and being influenced by them, dependent on them as they are dependent on us. We have roles to play in these many systems; there are stories unfolding and we have our parts in these continuing stories. Given this inexorable connectedness of system life, is freedom possible?

Freedom in systems is the ability to seize the opportunity of the moment, without being constrained by our role, our history, the expectations of others, or the pull of systemic conditions.

In the interconnectedness of system life there are many constraints that work against our seeing opportunities, let alone seizing them. There are the roles we play, which make certain acts acceptable and others unacceptable; seizing the opportunity may require that we step out of role. There is a momentum to system life, a direction in which things are moving; seizing the moment may require us to interrupt that momentum. We have a history in our systems in the context of which people have certain expectations of us; seizing the moment may require us to violate those expectations. There is the way things usually go in system life; seizing the moment may require us to break the pattern of the usual. Such freedom is a frightening possibility—to step out of role, to break with history, to violate the expectations of others, to go against the pull of systemic conditions. Acting with such freedom, one cannot help but appear strange to others, possibly dangerous, certainly a bit mad.

I experienced freedom when I canceled the future ("The First Encounter"), when I said to my children, "What's in it for me?" ("The First Encounter"), when I offered to switch from Coach to Middle ("One That Got Away"); I felt unfree in the minutes and hours before taking these actions, and I felt unfree when I recognized that I could have raised my hand when the Elite asked for volunteers ("One That Got Away"); I experienced freedom when I quit my Middle job, when my partner and I created Oasis, and when we begged for food ("Begging with Barry"). Such freedom is exhilarating and it's frightening; it sets you apart from others; and given that we are system creatures, apartness is unsettling for us and for them.

Such freedom is not freedom *from* systems. When system life becomes unbearable, freedom from systems is what members often seek. So long as we remain system members, there is no freedom *from*. We are still components of the whole, interdependent parts. Yet we are free *in* the system when we step out of the flow and seize the opportunity.

We Are Self-in-System Creatures

In system life there are many moments—some brief and some prolonged—in which we feel angry, weak, lost, frustrated, overwhelmed, and so forth. When we treat such experiences as personal, then the obvious solution is to work on ourselves. The alternative is to recognize that we are not merely isolated selves with our personal strengths and weaknesses, we are persons-in-systems, and that our experiences have something to do with the condition of our system and our relationship to it. Often our discomfort is not merely personal; it is a clue that something is amiss in the system. This was the case for me in "One That Got Away" when I volunteered to be a Middle. Again one might say that my midnight anxiety attack was a reflection of personal insecurity and that my self-confidence needed shoring up. The other interpretation is that my anxiety was a message that something was wrong with the system: there was no Middle, and that was having consequences for the whole system. One solution—there may have been many other alternatives—was to change my relationship to the system: *I'll be your (and the system's) Middle*. This was also the case with the discomfort that led to my canceling the future ("The First Encounter") and the frustration that led to my retirement ("Begging with Barry").

Either I am a neurotic, easily prone to anxiety attacks and in urgent need of repair, or I am a self-in-system creature who sometimes but not always trusts that my experiences are reflections of the condition of the system and my relationship to it. After the police came a second time (in the "Begging with Barry" tale), and I was feeling badly (cheating) taking food from the church, had I allowed that feeling to take hold—*Something is wrong about this*—listened to it as a message about my relationship to the system, and therefore refused to take the food from the church, might that not have gotten me closer to seeing my limit situation (continuing to beg *was* a possibility) and gotten me to face the choice of continuing or not?

The message in all of this is: We are not visitors to the system, we are part of it. It works us just as we work it. Our experiences are connected to the condition of the system and our relationship to it. Rather than fixing ourselves (or narcotizing ourselves against our feelings), we can change our relationship to the system. And by changing our relationship to the system, we change that system, sometimes in small ways and sometimes fundamentally.

Feel the System; Know the System

The message up to this point has been: Feel the system. Immerse yourself deeply in it; allow it to work you, and use your feelings as clues to the system's condition. Fix the system by fixing your relationship to it.

We've also alluded to the importance of system knowledge. Having a deep understanding of systems gives us a context for understanding our feelings; it provides a framework for connecting our personal feelings to the condition of the system. In "Begging with Barry" I was able to connect my feelings to my knowledge of middleness, and once the connection was made, certain action possibilities opened up for me. Without such knowledge you are left with the choices of bemoaning and trying to correct your personal weaknesses or feeling victim to the unfortunate conditions in which you find yourself. I once asked a colleague how he would have coached me in the "Begging with Barry" incident when I was a Middle and an Immigrant shouted across the room, "Barry, these rolls are hard!" He talked about working with me on my sensitivity to criticism, and working with the Immigrant on his reactions to me. And had all of that worked, newly sensitized me would have been able to continue in my Middle role. I experienced this incident against a different knowledge base; for me, this was simply one more incident in what was promising to be an endless dance of middleness. My partner and I were being held accountable (by both Elite and Immigrants) for matters that we didn't control. *Rolls were his problem, not mine. Keeping the Immigrants in line was the Elite's problem (they had created these conditions), not mine.* Why were the Immigrants, Elite, and I colluding in acting as if I were responsible for their issues? It was against that base of system knowledge regarding the nature of middleness that I stepped out of the flow and into the exhilaration and fear of freedom.

Sometimes when we are hit full force with the reality of our systemic nature, it strikes us not as a problem but as a joke. In one of our organization exercises, two Tops were talking about their difficult relationship. One turned to the other and said with some feeling, "You are a dictator!" And then they both had a big laugh remembering that just that morning, in another exercise, they had been Bottom teammates, and at that time they had talked about what a great team they were, how creative they were, and how well they got along. So what had happened in the course of a few hours? Was there some traumatic personal transformation? Clearly not. The two of them had moved from a Bottom space, which generated a predictable "WE-ness," to a Top space, in which they fell into equally predictable difficulties of directional differentiation—"We need to run the system this way." "No, we need to run it that way!" (See "The System Story I in Part II" and "Systemic Imbalance" in Part III.) In both exercises, their feelings toward one another felt solid, based on the "realities" of who they were as individuals. But how could that be?

One can find this story amusing, yet consider those Tops in organizations who have these same intense negative feelings toward one another; for them there is no laugh, no second exercise, no recognition of the systemic nature of their experience, no sense that had *they* been Bottom teammates, they too might have felt terrific about their creativity and their relationship.

And take this a step further. Consider all the negative feelings in the world—from indifference to hate—think of the righteousness of cold and hot wars, of culture wars, of inter- and intrareligious strife, holocausts, and ethnic cleansings. All these also proceed out of a solidity in our experiences. We can feel these ways about one another and do these terrible things to one another because of who we and these others are...*objectively*. Or so we think. How many of these "solid realities" are also systemic?

System knowledge is not easy to come by. Can the solitary ant understand the complex processes of the Hill, or the single bee comprehend the workings of the Hive? Can we humans comprehend the processes of the Wholes of which we are a part? That is the challenge.

Again, the Power Lab has been a great boon to me in this respect. When I have not been an active player in the society, I have been the detached observer of it. I have had the rare opportunity to stand aside system after system and view them as wholes.

These are two aspects of system mastery. In the one we immerse ourselves in the system; in the other we distance ourselves from it. In the one, we *feel* the system deeply; we allow it to work us, and we use our feelings as clues to the system's condition. In the other, we stand aside the system, we attend more to what we see than to what we feel; we observe the system, the whole of it: What is ITs shape, ITs functioning? How is IT stuck? What is IT missing?

The two roads connect. Knowledge contextualizes our feelings; feelings bring our knowledge to the fore.

In the next sections we are going to stand aside systems, see them as wholes, deepen our knowledge of them so when the moment of freedom comes, when it is time to seize the moment, we will recognize it and know what to do with it.

Part II

Lessons from the Outside

C H A P T E R

6

System Story I: The Predictable Lives of Tops, Middles, and Bottoms

Tolstoy suggested that all happy families are the same, but the unhappy ones are unhappy in their own unique ways. My experience tells me it is just the other way around: it is the unhappy (blind) systems that regularly fall into the same old predictable scenarios, and that only with system sight can one create uncharted futures.

Essential System Knowledge

Much of what I know about systems and the possibilities of system leadership stems from my many experiences as anthropologist at New Hope. In that role I have had the opportunity to stand aside system after system, witnessing the interactions within and across system lines, developing system knowledge essential to system leadership.

Although each Power Lab tells its unique story, there is also a System Story, an underlying story—a set of archetypal themes, tensions, relationship breakdowns—that carries throughout all labs, independently of who the players are. The System Story is not limited to the Power Lab; I believe you will recognize it in many of the systems of your life.

When we are living the System Story, it doesn't seem to us that we are simply running through the old familiar story again; to us our story feels unique, special, a function of the unique characteristics of the players involved and the particular circumstances we are in. There are many variations on the System Story, yet in essence it is always the same old story.

When we are blind to the System Story, our systems are destined to go on living it; the challenge of system leadership is to understand the System Story in a way that allows us to avoid it and create newer and and powerful stories for ourselves and our systems.

New Hope is one system, yet within that one system there are three very different systems, each existing in its own unique environment. Each environment creates unique issues and challenges for its members to face, and members tend to respond to these issues and challenges in fairly regular ways, producing their predictable System Story.

What is true for New Hope is true for all complex systems. It broadens our scope to see how the System Stories of New Hope play out in these other arenas as well.

The unique conditions the Elite in New Hope face are similar to those faced by those in other "Top" systems, that is, those who collectively have overall responsibility for a system—executives, business owners, parent couples.

The unique conditions the Immigrants face are similar to what is faced by those in other "Bottom" systems, those living in a world of shared vulnerability—workers in organizations and institutions, poor people in a neighborhood faced with the prospect of gentrification, a nation under threat of attack by another nation.

The conditions the Middles in New Hope face are similar to what is faced by those in other "Middle" systems, that is, systems whose members are pulled away from one another and out toward other individuals, groups, or activities—middle managers, supervisors, deans, department heads, neighbors in a suburban area.

System	Environmental Conditions	Examples
Top	Members are collectively responsible for the whole system, and they regularly are confronted with complex, difficult, and unpredictable issues.	New Hope Elite; top executive teams, parent couples, business partners.
Middle	Members are pulled apart from one another, out toward other individuals, groups, or activities.	New Hope Middles; peer groups of middle managers, supervisors, staff specialists; the deans and department heads in a university; neighbors in suburban areas.
Bottom	Members exist together in a condition of shared vulnerability	New Hope Immigrants; workers in organizations and institutions; neighborhoods threatened by gentrification; nations in danger of attack by other nations; doctors in health care systems; professors in universities.

The Elite (Top) Story:
Fear, Responsibility for the Whole,
Complexity, Difference

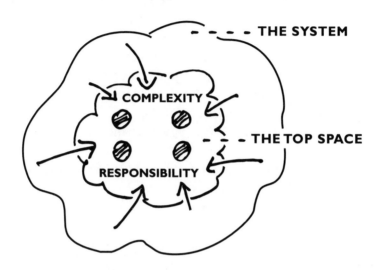

The Elite own New Hope. Theirs is a world of complexity and responsibility. The complexity is of two types: mastering what is given and creating what is not given. There are the many details of the Elite inheritance—the property, institutions, and traditions that go with their position. And then there are the challenges of creating what is not given; and as we shall see in the story to follow, there are endless choices and decisions to be made regarding the nature of that creation.

The Elite world is also a world of responsibility; as it is with the owners of a business, the executives of a corporation, the parents in a family, the Elite have overall responsibility for the traditions and operations of the system. For some Elite there is an added responsibility, the recognition that the success of the Power Lab as a learning event depends on their willingness and ability to be a powerful Elite with whom others must contend. If the Elite simply gave away all their resources and power, we all might have an interesting experience, but we wouldn't have the Power Lab. (By the way, if you are thinking that the Elite *should* give their resources away or at least share them with others, and you believe they are selfish, autocratic, and patriarchal if they don't, consider the implications of such thoughts for your own life. Do you own a home? Do you allow strangers in to share your property? Do you give them free rein with your refrigerator? Do they have the keys to your car? Access to your bank account? Do you involve them in democratic discussions regarding the use of your property? What makes many of our lives easier than those of the New Hope Elite is that, for many of us, we do not live nose-to-nose with the very people who would like greater involvement in decisions regarding our resources. If you give away your property in New Hope, chances are you never felt that you really owned it.)

So what are some themes we are likely to find in the Elite story regardless of who the Elite players are?

Fear

If you are not experiencing some degree of fear in the Elite position, some paranoia about sounds in the night, you are probably either numb or catatonic. There are sharp differences between you and others in regard to wealth and resource control, and you are not tucked away safely in some distant enclave. There are likely to be pressures on you to share your property and power, *and who knows what will happen to you if you don't?* One of the predictable themes centers around how the Elite handle their fear. Do they live with their fear or run away from it? Do they hide away or put themselves into the middle of the action? Do they tell the truth about their power or make believe (and make up stories) that they really don't have it? (Again, reader, you would do well to imagine yourself in these conditions. You own New Hope. You have and control what others don't have and don't control. Are you afraid, and how do you handle your fear?)

Homogenization and Differentiation (Tension over Turf or Consensus)

The Elite responsibilities are many and complex; there are numerous institutions to be maintained: work and pay, the judicial system, meals and housing, a newspaper, cultural activities, a store, a pub, recreational activities. One theme centers around how the Elite handle this complexity. Traditionally, each Elite has responsibility for a particular domain, but then the question arises: how independent will they be? At one extreme the Elite may attempt to homogenize their responsibilities—that is, they share all information and responsibilities and decide everything together. At the other extreme they may differentiate, with each Elite having sole control (and final say) over his or her domain. Either way raises predictable difficulties.

Extreme differentiation is likely to result in turf issues. New Hope is a system; policies and actions in one arena are likely to have implications for other arenas. If you are too giving (or withholding) in your arena, what pressures does this create for me in my arena? There are likely to be some inadvertent cross-territorial incursions, with some accompanying bad feelings.

On the other hand, extreme homogenization (a commitment to involvement and consensus on every issue) is likely to result in the Elites being swamped as unresolved complexities pile up at their door.

Differentiation (Directional)

The Elite have responsibility for the whole; there are likely to be differences regarding which direction the whole should take. *Should we involve others in major decisions, or do we reserve such decisions to ourselves? Do we give or withhold? Be tough or tender? Do we make life easy for folks or difficult? Do we empower them by giving them what they want, need, ask for; or do we empower them by making them struggle to get what they want, need, ask for?* Such directional differentiation struggles are likely to strike familiar chords with members of top executive teams, business partners, family couples—all of whom know the directional tugs that frequently arise in the top space.

Directional differentiations will occur. So if there is a hard-line Elite orientation, you can count on the eventual emergence of a soft-line orientation; if there is a cautionary Elite orientation, you can count on the eventual emergence of a more daring orientation. These directional differentiations are likely to be the most difficult issues the Elite face, tearing at their relationships with one another. The following are some of the forms this theme takes.

Endless bickering as members remain together while their relationship continues to deteriorate.

Sabotage as Elite undermine one another.

Avoidance, where the Elite stay at arm's length from one another, avoiding the tensions that would come from facing potentially divisive decisions, and then stepping on one another's toes as these independent actions intrude upon one another's turf.

Submergence, in which one or more of the Elite go along with the direction of others, never feeling fully at home with it, and behaving inconsistently, sometimes in accordance with the dominant mode and sometimes in opposition to it.

So each Elite story will be some variation on how the Elite handle fear and differentiation.

The Middle Story: Personal and Systemic Disintegration

ELITE

A
TEARING
WORLD

IMMIGRANTS

and

EMPLOYMENT

**FOOD AND
HOUSING**

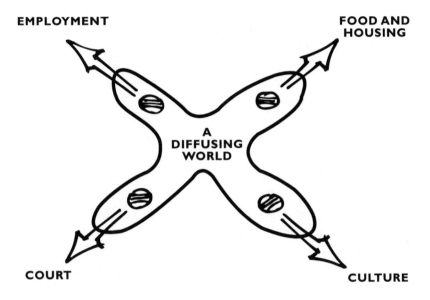

**A
DIFFUSING
WORLD**

COURT

CULTURE

The Middles enter an in-between world. They meet the Elite and learn that the Elite own everything; they learn that the Immigrants will soon be arriving and that they will own virtually nothing: little clothing, no guaranteed shelter or food, no money. They learn that the Middles are expected to run the Elite's institutions—employment, court, housing, meals, culture, information and entertainment—and that in return for such services, the Middles will be able to maintain a decent standard of living. They also learn that that standard of living is dependent on their accepting these managerial positions. Once having accepted these positions, the Middles find themselves interacting between two very different systems with markedly differing agendas. This is the up-and-down tearing (pulled between the Elite and the Immigrants) into which the Middles enter. (Some of you might be thinking that the courageous and moral thing to do would be to refuse the Middle job, with its salary and comforts, and cast your lot with the Immigrants. Once again, I suggest that you apply such thoughts to your current work and life situation.)

There is also a side-to-side tearing as the Middles, with their individual assignments, are regularly drawn apart from one another. One is busy with employment, another with food and housing, another with the court, still another with education and theater, and so forth. The assignments are distinct; the Middles report to different Elite, and there may be little that encourages mutual interaction and support.

Given these systemic conditions, the predictable themes in the Middle world are systemic and personal dis-integration.

Systemic Dis-integration. Two bases for what constitutes a system are: (1) there is a common mission, purpose, or function that connects all members; and (2) members support one another in the service of that mission, purpose, or function. According to these measures, the collection of Middles never becomes a system. Each has his and her function, but rarely (very rarely) is there a common Middle mission. As a consequence, Middles spend the bulk of their time handling their individual businesses and little or no time supporting one another. Notice that this is also not a bad description of many of our middle-class neighborhoods and many of our organizational middle-management peer groups.

Personal Dis-integration. Whereas in the Elite position, if you're not afraid, you're not paying attention; in the Middle position, if you're not confused, you're not paying attention. You are being pulled between two very different and conflicting systems, and there is a legitimacy to both of these systems. In what is perhaps an oversimplification, the Elite are for the most part a force for maintaining the overall system, the Immigrants are for the most part a force for changing the system, and you are attempting to function between the two. In this tearing place it is difficult to get grounded in your own solid position—what *you* think has to happen. Several times Middles have described their New Hope experience as "I wasn't there" or "I disappeared," meaning that as independent thinking individuals, with minds of their own, these Middles were not present.

In these middle conditions it is easy for you not to fully satisfy anyone; you're never quite strong enough for either the Elite or the Immigrants, and it is easy to internalize their dissatisfactions and consider yourself incompetent.

A Multiplier Effect

Personal dis-integration is reinforced by systemic dis-integration. In the absence of supportive system membership, each Middle faces these pressures, confusions, and self-doubts alone.

So the persistent theme of the Middle story centers around how each collection handles its dis-integration. Earlier, in reference to the Elite system, I mentioned how each system expresses its possibilities. Nowhere has this been more dramatic than in the Middle system. Time and again, not only has the Middle system disintegrated (or retained its initial dis-integrated state), but it has done so with perfect symmetry: when there were only three Middles, one Middle aligned with the Elite, one aligned with the Immigrants, and a third remained independent. (For two examples of this perfect symmetry, see "Bart and Barb" in *Seeing Systems* and "Last Hope, Lost Hope," the story to follow in Chapters 7 and 8.)

One can think of this symmetry as the Middle system expressing a range of possibilities for resolving personal dis-integration at the cost of complete system dis-integration. *I eliminate the tearing, confusion, self-doubts, and waffling by casting my lot with the Elite (align upward) or with the Immigrants (align downward), or by withdrawing from both (independence).* Whatever the limitations of these choices, they do serve to protect one's mental health. The Middle whose mental health is most vulnerable is the one who remains steadfastly stuck in the middle, attempting to please all sides, constantly falling short, yet valiantly charging ahead.

The Immigrant (Bottom) Story:
United Yet Different and Separate

"THEM"

SHARED VULNERABILITY

Immigrants enter New Hope with little more than the clothes on their back; they have no money, no guaranteed housing, no provisions for food or supplies. They quickly find themselves at an employment center, where they can sign up for work to earn some funds that will enable them to rent a bed, buy a meal, purchase supplies, and maybe not all of these at once. If Immigrants do sign up, the work they find is physical—maintaining or beautifying New Hope property; the pay is minimal, requiring them to make what may be difficult buying choices. The differences between their conditions and those of others are stark and plain to see—the food they can afford, their living conditions, their limited clothing, the nature of the work they do. The Immigrants live in a world of shared vulnerability: others—primarily the Elite, but also the Middles—make decisions affecting many aspects of their lives: housing, food, work, supplies, justice.

In response to these conditions, Immigrants quickly integrate; they become a unified system. They develop a WE (the Immigrants) versus THEM (the Middles and Elite...and sometimes the staff) mentality. They huddle together, sharing information and resources, making decisions together. There is a camaraderie within the group, a strength that comes from their togetherness.

In time, integration, which is the Immigrants' strength, exacts its toll. Differences begin to emerge within the Immigrant group. *Do we accept the system as given to us or do we challenge it? If we challenge it, do we do so through reasoned petitions and negotiations or through direct action? And is there any place for ME and my uniqueness in this WE? Does my commitment to the WE stifle my individuality?*

Once again, if we look at the Immigrant system as a whole, we see a system expressing its possibilities: the various positions the system could take, the various lives its members could live; and working against this elaboration of possibilities is the overriding pressure to maintain uniformity. So the theme of the Immigrant story is a system living in this tension between remaining integrated in the face of forces threatening to tear it apart: directional differentiations (does the WE go this way or that way?) and the pressures of individuation (members striving to be free of the group). Following are some of the ways in which this theme is played out:

Pressures toward uniformity. As directional differentiations develop, considerable energy is spent as each differentiated position attempts to convince the other of the correctness of its position. There can be prolonged, de-energizing, and futile debates, discussions, and arguments as the Immigrant system grinds itself into immobility.

Pressures toward conformity. If a dominant position does emerge within the Immigrant group, there is concerted effort to bring dissidents into line through debate, love, the threat of loss of membership, or force. Deviation is a threat to the dominants. On the one hand there is the fear of loss of uniformity and of a weakening, if not a dis-integration, of the system. And deviance has a subtler effect on the dominants; it threatens the validity of their position. *If we all agree, our position must be right;* but the very existence of deviance confronts us with a possibility we'd rather not face: the fallibility of our position.

Exile. When dissidents cannot be brought into the fold, they are ignored, treated as invisible, banned, jailed, or exiled. They are no longer part of the WE; they are now THEM.

Submersion. In order to maintain their position within the WE, members may hide their differences and go along reluctantly with the dominant direction. Shame is associated with such submersion—feelings of anxiety, weakness, cowardice. Sometimes members hide their difference from themselves; that is, they don't allow themselves to experience their difference and, as a consequence, sink into apathetic membership.

These, then, are the System Stories—the archetypal themes we find in all Elite (Top), Middle, and Immigrant (Bottom) systems independently of who the players are. Members enter the system and do what they do, unaware that they are falling into a relatively limited range of possible stories, unaware that they are living a familiar variation of the predictable Top, Middle, or Bottom story. Each system plays out its story uniquely, yet the range of variation is limited by the archetype.

Lessons

What am I seeing?

1. I am aware of how difficult it can be for us human beings to accept that we are living a System Story, to recognize that many of the deeply felt issues we are facing with one another are systemic rather than personal, that they are a consequence of the conditions we are in. What is it that we would have to give up? Our righteousness? Our sense of loss over what might have been had we been able to master the systemic conditions rather than fall victim to them?

2. So long as we remain blind to the archetypal stories, the familiar unhappy System Stories will recur. The "Begging with Barry" story offers the hope that with system knowledge, it is possible to break out of the archetype and create unfamiliar, unpredictable, and empowering System Stories. In subsequent sections we will explore other possibilities for recognizing and breaking out of the System Story.

◊

7

Last Hope, Lost Hope: Part I

(compiled by Barry and Karen Oshry and Joe Meier)

"So," God said..."What do you make of Me Who could have gotten it all right the first time, saved everyone and left Hell unstocked?...Why do I do it then? Why?"

"So we might choose," said one of the saved.

"Never," God thundered. "What do I care for the sanctity of your will? Never!"

"Goodness," a saint shouted. "You get off on goodness."

"On goodness? Me?" God laughed. "On goodness? Is that what you think?...Were you born yesterday?...Goodness?

"No. It was Art! It was always Art. I work by the contrasts and metrics, by beats and the silences. It was all Art."

"Because it makes a better story is why."

Stanley Elkin, *The Living End: A Triptych*

I'll Be Devoured

It is the first morning in New Hope. There is a community meeting scheduled for 11:30 A.M. The Immigrants will be looking for concrete outcomes. The Elite have a different view of the meeting: *We need to be clear; the meeting is merely for collecting data, not giving answers.* At 11:00 A.M. the Middles meet with the Elite and present a list of Immigrant "desires" they had compiled the previous night in the Pub. One item captures Elite Elizabeth's attention:

We want to experiment with the system.

Elizabeth: *Experiment with the system? This could be a violation of the law...actions aimed at overthrowing the social order.*

At the 11:30 meeting, the Immigrants express their feelings and make their demands: *The system keeps us in poverty....Nothing we do is worthwhile....We want fast action....You three (Elite) are ignorant....This is a place without justice....*Immigrant Brenda says: *I'm not recognizing that there are any Elite here...we are profoundly together on this.*

At lunch, the Elite discuss the community meeting. Elizabeth says: *It was a disaster. Nothing we do will be enough. There'll be endless sucking. I'll be devoured.*

(To be continued.)

A Story That Is Unique *and* Archetypal

This is my confession. As a longtime anthropologist of the Power Lab, for me it has always been the Art, the Story. People come to New Hope searching for experience, growth, learning. They hope to become better, wiser, more powerful. They struggle to find their places, their power; they do battle with one another and with themselves; they suffer their frustrations, their pain, their depressions; and they have their moments of exhilaration and experiences of breakthrough. I hope, and the staff and I do our best, to see that people find what they are looking for. But I am looking for something else. I trail along with my notebook, writing it all down, joining with the other anthropologists, absorbing their pieces of the whole, caught up in the story. The drama. It is the story that grabs me. It is always unique, a reflection of the unique characteristics of the players, the choices they make and their interactions with one another. At the same time, it is always an expression of the System Story and the archetypal themes regularly played out by the Elite (Tops), Middles, and Immigrants (Bottoms).

This is the story of one Power Lab. It is a rich story, yet no richer than that of other Power Labs. What is unique in this story is its detail. Over the years we have documented other labs, but this is the only society to date whose story we have pieced together from beginning to end. (The story as told here is abridged from the original document of more than 200 pages.) This was a labor of love for Karen Oshry, Joe Meier, and me. Each of us had hundreds of pages of notes; each of us had seen pieces of the whole but not the whole. For more than a year we met weekly at Northeastern University's faculty club, sharing the information we had, unraveling the society's story like a mystery, clue by clue.

Last Hope, Lost Hope is packed with events—confrontations, plots and counterplots, drama, hope, despair, betrayal, choices, honesty and deception, fear and bravery, yet it may surprise the reader to learn that all of this happened in little more than three days and with a cast of only thirteen players. In New Hope, for reasons we don't fully understand, much living is packed into a few short days. I think the reader will recognize how much this tiny society of thirteen people is a fractal of much larger systems, that the issues of this microcosm are the same issues faced in the macrocosm. (To make it easier for the reader to keep names straight, all Elite names begin with *E,* all Middle names with *M,* and all Immigrant names with B [we found *I* too limiting.]).

I suggest that you read this story against the background of the System Story (previous chapter). Enjoy the unique drama while at the same time seeing this story as one variation on the archetypal theme:

- the instant coalescence of the Immigrants in the face of their shared vulnerability, the powerful We versus Them mentality that develops, the pressures toward conformity within the group, the inevitable tensions that emerge as individual differences come up against pressures for uniformity;

- the perfect disintegration of the Middles, their perceived incompetence by all sides, their ultimate total fractionation—one up, one down, one out;
- the Elite deceptions as they attempt to cope with their fear, the directional differentiations that tear at them regarding the kind of Elite they want to be, and the submergence that occurs as one Elite's orientation conquers the others'.

I hope that in reading this story you will identify with people rather than evaluate them. Given the conditions into which they (and you) have been born, how would you have played out your life—as an Elite? Middle? Immigrant?

Back to the Beginning: The Elite Receive Their Inheritance

THE ELITE

Elizabeth

Ernest

Edie

Three people with very different personalities are entering this Top space. It is important to see how these differences play out over time. Early in their deliberations they share their images of themselves as Elite. Elizabeth sees herself as the Empress by birth and title, who maintains the family line and her position through maturity. Ernest says, *I have inherited a system I do not agree with.* He wants to be accepted as the one with the history and knowledge about the society and its future. He talks about feeling a heavy responsibility for making this society work for everyone. Edie says, *This has been given to me. I haven't earned it. I would give it away and then work my way up to it.*

The Elite receive their inheritance—the resources they control and the institutions for which they are responsible. They learn about the stark distinctions between their conditions and those of the Immigrants. Elizabeth: *All my egalitarianism is shot to hell.* Ernest: *I'd like to see if I can tolerate the differences; I don't know if I can.*

There is the question of how the Elite present themselves to the rest of society. Elizabeth wants to create a mythology with magical names; Edie disagrees: *I'm going to call myself Edie.*

There are prolonged and recurring discussions regarding what to do about luggage. (On entering the society, the Immigrants surrendered most of their belongings—their money, credit cards, car keys, and most of the clothing they brought with them.) The Elite control these items and they wrestle with the question of how to deal with them. Should we sell the luggage, give it back, put it in the store, deny that we have it? Edie: *We could put our cards on the table...tell them that we control the luggage and that we're willing to negotiate.* Elizabeth disagrees: She does not want the Immigrants to know they control the luggage. *Sometimes we'd have to be autocratic,* she says.

Blankets become an issue; Immigrants may not have enough funds to buy them. Ernest: *Just give them the blankets!* Elizabeth: *For nothing?*

There is the question of how much control to exert over the Middles, and related is the matter of how much money to turn over to them. Edie proposes giving them $1,500 NH (New Hope)—which is a considerable chunk of the New Hope treasury—as a sign of good faith, an investment in community. Elizabeth strongly disagrees, concerned that they would no longer have control over whether or not this would be an egalitarian society. Ernest accuses Elizabeth of suffering from paranoia!

(Early on there is the tension (directional differentiation)—most clearly between Elizabeth and Edie—regarding what kind of a system the Elite want this to be. Elizabeth's view will prevail, and Edie will find herself going along with that view, sometimes comfortably, sometimes not.)

The Middles Arrive, Then the Immigrants, and the Struggle Over the Life of the System Begins in Earnest

---

THE MIDDLES:

Mitch

Maureen

Micky

The Middles arrive. There are three managerial positions to be filled: the heads of employment, facilities, and police. There is some confusion, and then tension, among the Elite as to how the Middles are to be slotted. The Elite had agreed that they themselves would make the final decisions, but then Edie tells the Middles that they can decide among themselves.

Maureen becomes manager of employment, Micky is manager of facilities, and Mitch is chief of police.

The Middles learn about the conditions into which the Immigrants will arrive. Micky: *There'll be a union formed real quick.* Micky: *Without a blanket there's no way to stay warm,* to which Edie replies, *There's heat in the building.* After a brief orientation by the Elite, the Middles are given the responsibility for orienting the Immigrants.

(Early on, of the three Middles, Micky stands out as the one who empathizes most strongly with the Immigrants' condition. We will see how that kindliness plays out in the Middle space.)

THE IMMIGRANTS:

Bob

Bud

Bernie

Betsy

Benjamin

Brenda

Brother Bart
(spiritual advisor to the community)

The Immigrants arrive.

They are a feisty bunch who—with the exception of Bud—have little enthusiasm for the work they are given and are quick to give the Middles and the Elite a hard time. At pay time they pool their money to make purchases at the store: six Class B breakfasts, six rents, two tubes of toothpaste, etc.

The court meets for the first time, with Chief Justice Elizabeth presiding. There is a struggle over how the benches are to be arranged: the Immigrants rearrange them to form a circle; the Elite insist that they be put back in courtroom style. The Immigrants use the court session as an opportunity to express their complaints: unequal food, no participation. Brenda: *I'm not recognizing that there are any Elite.* Bob: *I feel violence being done to me. This is a place without justice.* Elite Elizabeth: *Why don't you communicate your concerns to (Middle) Mitch?*

Meanwhile, the Elite, in their ongoing concern regarding how to handle the luggage situation, come up with a new scenario: *It has been lost at the border; we'll do what we can to get your things back.*

Later that evening, at the pub, Immigrants express their dissatisfactions and desires to Mitch, who agrees to represent them at the next morning's meeting with the Elite. Meanwhile the Elite continue to wrestle with their ambivalence. Ernest: *Yesterday we were talking about the good society. Today most people see us as a law-and-order society.*

Before the morning work session, the Immigrants consider their options: a mock burial of the society, a strike, take over the dining room, sit at the Elite table.

(What is unique about the Immigrant group is its almost complete rejectionist stand right from the beginning. In other New Hopes one finds stronger voices for moderation, a greater willingness to work within the system. Here there is little of that. We don't hear Betsy's voice often, but when we do, it is that voice of moderation.)

Saved by the Parallel Organization

That afternoon a continuation of the community meeting reinforces Elizabeth's fears of "endless sucking." Bob wants money for Class A meals and to "have a little left over." Bud wants the work to be better organized. Brenda wants a common work pool of *all* members, including the Elite. Bob feels the society could do away with the Middles. Brenda: *We're not threatening your authority...not at this point, in any case.* Bob: *We don't like that we serve you and we don't get served.* And on it goes until Benjamin proposes the idea of a Parallel Organization—that is, keeping the present structure intact while creating a new structure. Bob assures the Elite that this would be very safe for them—*You can keep everything you've got.* The Parallel Organization would have representatives from each part of the system, and if a consensus were developed among the representatives, it would be brought to the Elite for approval. The idea is very appealing to the Elite. *That's interesting,* says Ernest. *Very interesting,* says Elizabeth. The Elite agree to give the Parallel Organization the highest priority. At dinner that evening the Elite are feeling greatly relieved. Edie: *There is no way they were going to take the society and destroy it.* Elizabeth: *When I ask myself what is the bottom line—who keeps control?—I get clear and back on track.*

What About Us?

Initially the Middles are enthusiastic about the prospects of a Parallel Organization, then concerns set in. They demand a meeting with the Elite. Maureen takes the lead. *We see (the Parallel Organization) as a grave threat to society....The Immigrants will be managing themselves....They don't have the ability....You will be at their mercy....*She touches on the Elites' worst fears. *You may find yourselves digging flower beds while the Immigrants are making policy.* Maureen insists that the Middles be given full authority to run the society while the Elite function as strategists. The Middles also demand full disclosure of all information—finances, the luggage situation, and so forth. The Middles pledge their complete commitment to the Elite principles. There is a final demand. Maureen: *The next meeting is at your home* (the location of which the Elite have been keeping under wraps).

How Full Is Full Disclosure?

The Elite's initial reaction is negative. *We can't go along,* says Ernest, *they're asking for full disclosure.* Edie suggests that they fully disclose a myth. The Elite concoct a complex story regarding the intricacies of their financial situation. They call in the Middles, tell them that they accept their proposal, and proceed with "full" disclosure. *We're laying our cards on the table,* says Edie. Mitch and Micky are so pleased about the full disclosure that they pay little attention to detail, but Maureen tries very hard to understand. *It's still not clear to me,* she says. She assumes there must be some simple explanation for her confusion. Maybe it's math anxiety, maybe Edie isn't explaining it clearly, maybe it's the lateness of the hour. It doesn't occur to her that her confusion about the money picture is an accurate reflection of the fact that the explanation is bogus. So much for full disclosure.

I Don't Do Suitcases

Micky has a new lease on life. Mitch is to be the Middles' representative at the Parallel Organization, so Micky becomes the new work supervisor. His intention is to do something positive for the Immigrants right off. He plans to buy some new underwear to sell in the New Hope store. He comes to the Immigrants' breakfast table, explains his plan, and asks everyone for their underwear sizes.

Brenda: (affronted) *I won't give you my underwear size.*

Betsy: (to the others) *Why don't we just go on washing out our underwear daily?*

Brenda: (to Micky) *Why just underwear?*

Micky: *If you want more, you'll have to ask.*

Bud: (angry) *Do I have to tell you?…We want our luggage!*

Micky: (seeing his well-intentioned plan going down in flames) *I don't know if we have as many options about luggage.*

Brenda: (with sarcasm) *Thanks, Micky, we'll get back to you.*

Micky leaves. *This is a bad start to a day that will only get worse for him.*

To Work or Not to Work?

The agreement was that the society would continue while the Parallel Organization met, but the Immigrants are not sure whether they want to sign up for work. The Elite were to get back to them the night before with information, which they failed to do. And then there was that humiliating underwear business with Micky. They drift up to the employment center, still uncertain as to whether they will work. They find a poster indicating that they have been given a raise and that there is now one class of meals, intermediate in price and quality to the old Class A and Class B. The time to begin work has passed. Middle Maureen is pressing them for a decision. Brenda: *I say we don't work.* For Betsy the issue is not so clear. *Shouldn't we work while the Parallel Organization goes on?* She thinks for a moment. *Or should we?* She thinks again. *After all, we are making $1.50 an hour more.* Brenda: *They're keeping us in the same position.* Benjamin: *We're expecting them to change overnight.* Betsy: *Is it possible they made those changes with good intent?* Brenda: *No.* The Immigrants agree not to work, and head off to the beach instead.

End Terrorism and Then There Will Be Peace or, Make Peace and That Will End Terrorism

The Parallel Organization—Edie for the Elite, Benjamin for the Immigrants, and Mitch for the Middles—had been meeting all morning. The bulk of the interaction has been between Benjamin and Edie, and much of the morning has been spent on the "antisocial" actions of the Immigrants: stealing fruit, confiscating the candles and candle holder from the Elite table, and now not working after having agreed to work. Neither party denies the antisocial behavior; to Edie it is evidence of Immigrant irresponsibility; to Benjamin it is evidence that the Elite/Middle structure has failed.

A second theme has to do with *Who decides?* Edie refers to the changes the Elite have already made. Benjamin dismisses those as Band-Aids: *Changes like that should be made in a collective manner.* He complains that food and clothing are basics: *You're asking us to pay for these in bits and pieces; they should be givens.* Edie: *Is that real, that basics should be given? Is that what we should have—a welfare state?* Benjamin presses for tangibles—food, lodging, clothing. Edie: *We could purchase some things the Immigrants need.* Benjamin: *That's the same old system:* you *decide what to purchase. What if your resources were turned over to the community?* Edie: *You're asking for carte blanche...an entirely new system. We have no evidence that would justify such a change. We don't see any good intentions out there.* And then, as if to underscore Edie's point, in walks Bernie; he says nothing, simply sits down as if to observe. Edie protests: *This is now a fishbowl...a game; I don't want to play games.* Benjamin eventually asks Bernie to leave, which he does, and then the conversation reverts to "antisocial" actions—to Edie they are evidence of Immigrant irresponsibility; to Benjamin they are evidence that the Elite/Middle structure has failed, and on it goes.

Micky's Day Darkens

It is near lunchtime; Micky interrupts the Parallel Organization meeting and says, *I need to give the kitchen a lunch count.* The Immigrants have not worked nor signed up for lunch; the

Elite and Brother Bart simply get their lunches without paying for them. All Micky needs to know is whether Mitch and Benjamin, who are working in the Parallel Organization, will have lunch. The situation gets more complicated as Benjamin responds quickly, *Assume that all the Immigrants will want lunch.* But they haven't worked, and they haven't signed up for lunch. Benjamin figures maybe he can get paid for his work with the Parallel Organization and buy the Immigrants' lunch. He leaves to see if the Immigrants want lunch.

Meanwhile, the Immigrants have been hardening in their anti-Elite resolve. They say they want lunch but *with no strings.* Benjamin returns to the Parallel Organization to negotiate for his salary. Edie is stunned. *A fair compensation for our time together should include payment for everyone's lunch? Don't you see this as blackmail?* Benjamin insists. He tells Micky he is ordering lunch for all the Immigrants. Edie suggests that Benjamin sign an IOU, which he does. So now the Immigrants will have lunch, and Benjamin owes the society $18. Benjamin, feeling pleased with himself, reports back to the Immigrants. He thinks he is bringing a hard-fought gift, but that is not how it is received. Bernie says, *That's a string; we said no strings.* And Brenda says, *Then I don't want to eat.*

Micky leaves the Parallel Organization meeting feeling relieved. Originally he was to have given the kitchen count by 11:00 A.M; he asked for a 30-minute extension, and now he is even late on that. It is 11:43, but at least it's settled. He gives the count: *Everyone will be eating.* But it's not over yet.

Micky meets Maureen on the green; he tells her that lunch is settled. *That's outrageous,* she says. *The Parallel Organization can't do that. All they can do is recommend.* According to last night's agreement between the Elite and the Middles, this was a decision for the Middles, not one for the Parallel Organization. For Maureen the issue is clear: whether the Immigrants eat is determined by the existing structure, not by the Parallel Organization. According to the existing structure, you eat by paying for meals, and you earn money by working. The Immigrants did neither; therefore they don't eat. Once more to the kitchen goes Micky. *The count now is seven,* he says. *Who's not eating?* he is asked. *All the Immigrants,* he answers. Micky is feeling devastated; he returns to the Parallel Organization accompanied by Maureen. He tells them the latest decision. Benjamin is stunned. *Understand what you are doing,* he says. *My credit is good.* He asks again, *Will you accept my credit?* Maureen and Micky say *No.* They exit; then Micky returns. One more question: *Benjamin, would you like to eat lunch?* Benjamin gives a resounding *NO!* Edie says, *I will not eat lunch either.* And Mitch says, *Nor will I.* Micky finds Elizabeth and Ernest; he informs them that the Parallel Organization is not eating. Ernest is very upset with both Maureen and Micky. He turns to Micky and says, *Go to the kitchen! Tell them that there will be five for lunch*—Ernest and Elizabeth, Micky and Maureen, and Brother Bart. So much for Middle autonomy.

Just What Is the Parallel Organization?

It is lunchtime. Elizabeth and Ernest are having lunch at the Elite table. Ernest is upset at Edie for not coming to lunch. Micky and Maureen are joined by Brother Bart at the Middles' table. And in another cottage, the Parallel Organization continues its work. The Parallel Organization means different things to different people. To its members it is a significant entity; it may be the last hope for developing an integrated society. To Middles Maureen and Micky it is a threat to their position. To the Elite it is a committee of theirs (they have even begun referring to it as the Planning Committee) rather than a Parallel Organization; to them it is merely a recommending body that, unless it goes out of control, should pose no threat to them. To the Immigrants it is nothing; it is one of a number of relics of a society that no longer exists.

The Seeds of a New Society Are Planted

For while the Parallel Organization was meeting, the Immigrants were making plans to create their own independent society—the New Society. Bud had been exploring possibilities for bringing food into the New Society. While the Parallel Organization was wrestling with the lunch issue, the Immigrants were establishing the principles of their new world. *We will create our own money....All spaces will be open at all times....The basics of food, clothing, and shelter are available....We include all citizens in forming the society....We create autonomous (unsupervised) work teams....We print our own money....All of us (including the Elite and Middles) determine who will participate....We have a common eating space....We have a shared mechanism for handling justice....All menial tasks are shared among all members....We set aside time for leisure.* As the Immigrants pull further and further away from New Hope, they become protective against all outsiders, including the staff.

Put Yourself in Their Shoes

Micky and Maureen are walking and talking. Micky talks about how hard it was for him being squeezed from all sides. *It's easy for them to say 'We changed our minds,' but I'm the one who had to resolve it.* Micky has some empathy for the Immigrants' situation. *Put yourself in their shoes,* he says. Maureen's reply: *I'm having trouble doing that.*

Do We Break Off All Ties?

In the list of principles for the New Society that the Immigrants were drawing up, the last item, initially proposed by Bud, is now in boldface: **That we break off all ties with the old society.** Bernie doesn't buy it. *We must stay true to our principle of honest, open communication.* He is concerned about deceiving the Elite into thinking that the Immigrants are still in the society (given their continuing representation in the Parallel Organization) when in fact they are out. Bob is not troubled about deception; the Elite's actions justify any deception he might engage in. Bud is impatient with Bernie's reasonableness. *We are no longer accessible. Negotiations are over!* Brenda supports the notion of a clean break. This is too much for Bernie. *Where do you draw the line? How would we ever know if they were to open to real change?* The Immigrants continue to explore possibilities for finding ways of working for food. Betsy raises questions regarding securing their building. *We need to have someone here,* she says. *No,* says Bob, *if they take our beds we take theirs.* Bernie says, *But that would be violence.* Bob says, *Violence to property is not beyond me.*

An Attempt to Overthrow the Government

The Parallel Organization continues to slog on with its work. It comes up with a new structure for the society, complete with steering committees for work, communications, compensation, personal growth and development. And Benjamin throws another item in: "Enablers," without which he feels the plan will not fly. Enablers include such items as free sheets, pillow cases, and lodging for all; clothing for all who want it; and free meals for the next 24 hours. Edie is shocked. *We've already given, and what do we get? No work. I give but I get nothing in return.* Benjamin says, *Work will get done when we are treated like adults.* Edie: *You want compensation for nothing, for not working?* The allotted time for the Parallel Organization is over; according to plan, the results are to be brought to the Elite for discussion. Although Edie has sizable reservations regarding these Enablers, both she and Benjamin feel they have made progress.

Edie brings the proposal to the Elite. Elizabeth: *This is an attempt to overthrow the government.* Ernest: *They want everything at once.* Elizabeth: *It bothers me that you and Mitch would bring us such a thing.* Ernest is concerned that if the Elite take too hard a stand, *we will blow this apart.* He is ready to take a more conciliatory position. *Are they really asking for a lot? They are not asking for our house; they are not asking to take away our belongings.* Elizabeth assures him that the Immigrants are asking for quite a lot. *They are wiping out the social order,* she says.

We Will Have to Forget the Middles

Dinnertime approaches. There is the question of whether the Elite should provide dinner, an indication that they are accepting some of the enablers. There is also the question of who decides. Hadn't the Elite turned over responsibility for day-to-day running to the Middles? Ernest feels that was a mistake. *When (the Middles) changed their jobs around, it all went to zero.*

Elizabeth agrees. *The Middles were very ineffective today.* The dining room presses for an answer. *We will have to forget the Middles,* says Ernest. *Dinner for all.*

Is This Good News?

Benjamin brings the Immigrants the Elite response: dinner tonight, we can sleep in our house (not having paid rent), linens, and payment plans to be determined later by a steering committee of the Parallel Organization. Is this good news or not? Brenda thinks not. *What are we supposed to do,* she says, *be grateful?* Bob thinks otherwise. *This is a real breakthrough.* He tells Benjamin, *Go slow, play stupid, and have the Elite feed us forever.* Brother Bart elevates the significance of the choice. *I am interested in seeing how one meal can invigorate you so much. They keep you in the process with this one meal. You can put enormous pressure on them by not participating in the Parallel Organization structure tonight...and by not eating that meal.* Brenda agrees. *They are stringing us along with a crumb!*

Benjamin is exasperated. In his prolonged negotiations, he has by some standards won a considerable victory; yet it does not appear to be enough. *Where do you want me to draw the line?* he asks. *Don't you understand,* says Brenda, *we want guaranteed meals. We don't want to be negotiated for.* Benjamin: *I brought you 24 hours of meals; is that not good enough?* Both Bud and Brenda answer, *No, that is not good enough.*

Betsy says, *Haven't we changed the rules of the game? Yesterday we didn't ask for guaranteed food and housing.* Brenda: *That was our mistake.* There is no further discussion as to whether to accept dinner, but the dinner hour slips away as the Immigrants continue their deliberations.

Maureen on the Edge

At dinner, Maureen expresses the depth of her annoyance: *I feel betrayed by the Elite. We've worked hard to maintain their work ethic...and then they just give away this dinner!* She talks about the possibility of resigning and *sleeping on the floor if I have to.* She's tired of the Elite acting as if the Middles didn't exist.

We Are Dead

As the dinner hour slips away, the Immigrants are at logger-heads. Benjamin feels that a meeting of the total community is needed. Bud says he won't go to any meeting unless he is first guaranteed food and lodging. Brenda says they could use such a meeting to get their message across. Bud says, *I wouldn't even bother to go.* Brenda is hungry; she admits, *Dinner would be nice, but what kind of a statement does that make?* Betsy is still puzzled about where this hard-line Immigrant position came from. *We always told them that we'd be willing to work within the structure.* Benjamin suggests that they go to the dining room at the end of the hour. He says, *I have trouble with our attempting to create change by hibernating in a closet.* Bob suggests that they deliver a message to the Elite at dinner: *that basic necessities—like meals—are not a gift; they are a RIGHT!* Betsy says, *If dinner is a right, why are we treating it as a gift? Let's go get it.* Bernie says, *I want to go to dinner. I'm willing to deliver that message.* Brenda shocks Bernie by saying, *I don't trust you to make that statement. I prefer all of us go and convey the message.* Bernie says, *Frankly, I'm more interested in getting food than conveying a message.* The conversation continues; no suggestion has sparked general agreement. *We are dead,* says Bernie, *we have no energy.*

If You're Not Part of the We, You're Part of Them

Bit by bit, food has been coming into the Immigrants' cottage—wine, candy bars, pizza. Evidently the Immigrants have found some way to bring in food from sources outside of New Hope. When an anthropologist, who is attempting to document the history of the society, asks where the food comes from, at first there is no answer; and what answers do come, come reluctantly. The Immigrants are wondering: have they gone beyond the limits of the program using "outsider" people and "outsider" resources, and if the anthropologists knew about this, would they stop it? So at this point there is a great deal of secrecy about the Immigrants' eating plans.

It's Not My Fault They Left the Safe Open

Brenda comes in with another pile of merchandise from the store. She blames the Middles for her theft. *They did a lousy job of securing the store.*

A New Society Has Been Formed

Benjamin meets with the Elite. This is when the Elite are to respond to the Parallel Organization's decisions. The first items are agreed upon quickly: that all decisions of the Parallel Organization and its committees be made by consensus. The Elite press Benjamin to be sure he understands that that gives the Elite veto power. Benjamin assures them that he understands. There is also agreement on having a general community meeting. Then the matter of the Enablers comes up. Mitch reads the list. *Where are you on these?* asks Benjamin. Elizabeth says, *It does not work out right now. No work was done. And no food was eaten.* Elizabeth's position is that the Elite provided dinner even if the Immigrants chose not to eat. *We made the investment in dinner,* she says, *so in a sense you owe us.* Benjamin says, *Then there is nothing more to negotiate.* He drops his bombshell: *A new society has been formed.*

Where Will the Middles Go?

Mitch tells Maureen and Micky of Benjamin's announcement. His thought is that the Middles are forced to choose between the old society and the new one, and his choice is clear: *We have made a firm commitment to the existing society.* Micky is not so sure. *Maybe I would join that (the New) society.* And Maureen has still another vision: *There is no New Society. The Immigrants have just organized themselves in another way. This is where our Immigrants are now; we do not have to accept their vision.*

We Own That Land

Brother Bart is counseling the Elite. He tells them how solid the Immigrants are feeling. *The ground rules have changed,* he says. *It's more like negotiations among equals,* Elizabeth says, *but there is one essential factor—we own the property they are living in. Are we supposed to provide housing for their New Society? We built that place; we own the land.* Brother Bart: *It sounds like the story of the Indians, and they ended up with nothing.*

The Elite spend the next hour exploring their options: join forces, reintegrate the Immigrants into a remodeled New Hope Society, coexist as two separate societies, evict them. In the end, largely at Elizabeth's direction, the decision is to recognize the New Society.

Neither...Nor

Elizabeth and Maureen join a seminar initiated by the New Society. Elizabeth reads a statement recognizing the existence of the New Society. Maureen expresses her disagreement. She wants *all to become one society. I am no longer a part of the New Hope Society, and I am not part of the New Society.*

And the Work Goes On

Edie and Ernest hire two Craigville groundskeepers to do some work for them, and tell Mitch and Micky that they can manage these new Immigrants.

The Bill

Edie and Ernest decide to send the New Society a bill for using Elite housing. Mitch and Micky see them preparing the bill.

Micky: *Stop! Edie, I want to know what you are doing.*

Ernest: *What do you want to know?*

Micky: *Everything.*

Ernest: *We are writing a bill. We have been too lenient.*

Edie: *We are not into war. They may not pay, but this makes a demand on them.*

Mitch: *We should cease and desist right now! We started out with too much disparity between the classes. That drove us (Middles and Elite) together, but it drove them out. And this bill is headed toward driving them out of this society.*

Ernest: *We're willing to have them buy the house. All we're saying is, 'Here is the bill for what is due.'*

Ernest explains that the Elite are hiring new Immigrants and will need the money to pay them.

Mitch: *They will see it as a move to evict them. It adds up to moving toward a new Immigrant group.*

Ernest: *No, it's more like getting temporary help.*

Edie: *We have acknowledged their New Society and we want to open communications with them.*

Mitch: *This is not the way to do it!*

Edie says that Mitch and Micky are making too much of this. *A bill is only a bill.*

Micky: *You're right, but as an Immigrant I would react violently.*

Mitch suggests contracting with the Immigrants.

Edie: *Under our system, they are supposed to work.*

Mitch: *But is your system working?*

Ernest: *It has not collapsed yet. We can go outside and hire part-time Immigrants. Our bottom line with the Immigrants is: This bill has to be paid.*

Micky: *Even at the expense of breaking down all communication?*

Edie: *They owe the money. That is a fact. How they deal with this is up to them. We have already decided to hire part-time Immigrants. Let them cope. They can be creative; we can make our moves.*

Micky reads the notice. *You're giving them until noon. That's a hard line!*

Ernest: *You handle it.*

Micky: *Or we come up with some other way of handling it.*

Edie: *OK, as long as you take responsibility for what you do.*

So now the matter of the bill is in the Middles' hands.

Then We'll Just Have to Help Ourselves

It is lunchtime. The New Society people head for the dining room. If there is food for them, they will take it; if not, they will continue to provide for themselves. Brenda tells the dining room hostess that she wants a tray of food. The hostess replies, *I take my orders from the Elite.* Brenda takes a bowl of fruit. *Then we'll just have to help ourselves.* After lunch she runs over to the Elite cottage and "liberates" more supplies. *If they're dumb enough to leave their door open, then that's their problem.*

The Bill by Other Means

The Elite and Middles meet. There is agreement that merely presenting the bill for housing to the New Society would be inflammatory. A subtler plan is concocted. In the morning Bud had conducted a New Society seminar demonstrating a particular problem-solving model. What if the Elite proposed using that model to work on the society's current situation? The goals would be: (1) to have the New Society recognize the New Hope Society, and (2) to deal with the issue that the New Society is living in Elite-owned housing. Elizabeth's bottom line: *They need to be aware they are on our premises. We recognized them; now they have to recognize us. If they don't, they'll have to leave.*

The New Society agrees to use the problem-solving model to examine their current situation. Brenda and Benjamin are very uncomfortable about this. Brenda: *I don't want to use the seminar to negotiate issues.* And Benjamin's mood is cautious: *There's something too open-ended about this.*

The problem-solving meeting of the whole goes ahead. Early on, Elizabeth presses for recognition of the New Hope Society. Brenda resents the question. *That's not what this meeting is about.* But Elizabeth persists; for her that is precisely what this meeting is about. Bud says he acknowledges the existence of the New Hope Society. Elizabeth presses on. *Are we talking abstractly, or are we talking about our situation? If this is just abstract, then I'm not interested.* Again it is Bud who assures her that this is not abstract, that it is about the New Hope Society and the New Society. Elizabeth asks, *Is this agreed upon?* Brenda is stuck. Left to her own devices, she might not agree, but Bud has spoken, so how to deal with that? Brenda agrees, but does so in a manner as if nothing new has been established. *That was clear this morning,* she says dismissively.

A process is developed for exploring the meaning of "integration." It is a long process, in all taking over three hours. Bud, alone among the New Society, seems involved; it is his process and he has an investment in seeing it done well. Elizabeth, too, remains energized as she sees the process edging closer to the point she wants to make: *the New Society is living on Elite-owned property.* For others, particularly Benjamin and Brenda, the process has gone well out of control; it is beginning to look like the negotiations they were committed to avoiding.

The process finally yields the three most important integration processes: pool and share resources; provide subsistence for all persons; and acknowledge current space, land, and resources for each society.

Brenda at last stops the process. *Why are we doing this? This process is forcing integration.* Now the conversation turns to whether or not to proceed. Bud throws up his hands in frustration and leaves, done in as much by his own group as anything.

Elizabeth is frustrated. *When I started the meeting, it was agreed we were moving to action. Now you are saying that this is not true? Is this discussion supposed to be purely academic?* Brenda says, *Yes,* and Benjamin agrees.

Just before the meeting breaks up, Elizabeth, still having the bill on her mind, says, *There are issues that need to be addressed between the New Society and the New Hope Society.*

Let Us Share Our Visions...and That's All!

The society—or two societies—are stuck. The New Society members feel that their own seminar process has been used against them. Bud has already left; he wants no further contact with New Hope. Elizabeth and Ernest are not about to let go, although for different reasons. Ernest hangs on to his feelings of responsibility for creating a society that works for all; Elizabeth wants to build on the New Society's recognition of New Hope. So she and Ernest, working in tandem, offer a new plan. There is to be a one-hour meeting of the two societies. One person from each society will speak. The purpose is to share a sense of each society's current realities: who the members are, how they function, and the problems they face.

Benjamin shakes his head. Brenda at first says no. Her preference is for the New Society to continue its seminars. When Elizabeth presses her, Brenda agrees that the coming together would be useful *only if it is strictly factual and not for the purpose of change*. But now Bernie disagrees; he sees nothing wrong with the possibility of change or of the two societies influencing one another. He cautions Brenda, *I think we should speak individually*. Brenda looks ruefully at him and says, *We can talk about this in our group*.

Ernest asks if there is agreement on the plan, but the New Society is so fractionated at this point that there is no clear answer. Elizabeth asks, *Everyone will be here?* Benjamin answers, *Unless people elect not to be here*.

Do You Feel Powerful?

The Elite are discussing the upcoming session. Edie is unenthusiastic; she sees no purpose to it. And there is something missing for Ernest. He is wondering whether it's right for the Elite to stick to their structure. But Elizabeth is in a completely different place; she is relishing the significance of the "Integration Seminar." *They lost their vision, their sense of purpose. They unwittingly went along with our power move — the reassertion of society. Until now, we never forced them to face the reality that we exist.* We're really in this! *We exist, and we own this place. We need to point out the fact that the New Hope Society recognizes a need for change while recognizing the fact that people are living on our property in a way that is not feeding our society.*

Neither Ernest nor Edie shares Elizabeth's enthusiasm. Ernest asks Elizabeth, *Do you feel powerful?* and Elizabeth replies quickly and clearly, *Yes!* Ernest asks the same question of Edie, who, after some hesitation, replies, *Well, I don't feel powerless.* And although Ernest does not answer his own question, it is clear what his answer would be.

I Am with You…So Far

In the New Society there is much self-recrimination for having stumbled blindly into the integration process. There is anger at Bud for having recognized the New Hope Society so quickly and for allowing integration to become the subject of the seminar. Bud wants to have no further contact with New Hope; Brenda is clear that she wants to spend no further time negotiating; Betsy agrees. The general feeling is that the New Society must separate, it must sever all connection with New Hope, and work on developing its own possibilities. That is the general feeling but not the uniform one. Bernie disagrees; he is still searching for possibilities for everyone—which includes those other folks his people are committed to shunning. There is a stuckness here; there is a commitment among the members of the New Society to being a powerful WE, but what happens when there is fundamental disagreement regarding which way the WE should proceed—as is the case at this moment? Bernie is contemplating a venture of his own; it is at odds with the commitment of his group. How free does he feel to air his difference and pursue it? Will he lose his place in the New Society, a place he deeply values? Are others also feeling bound by the WE?

The question comes up: *Can we be an integrated* WE *and at the same time pursue our individual directions?* The conversation appears to bring new life to the New Society. Benjamin says, *I can support all of you, whether you mediate, negotiate, or whatever. We are tight enough to support each other whatever we do.* The New Society members relish this new spirit of independent togetherness—that there are many directions that could be pursued, that individuals are free to pursue these directions, while others support—or at least not constrain—them.

For Bernie this means the freedom to pursue alone his goal of "transcending what is." For Brenda this means putting together a dynamic presentation of who they are, going over there and delivering it, *and not getting caught up in their dealing with us.* For Betsy and Benjamin, this means supporting Brenda in making her presentation, going with her as she delivers it, even though both would prefer to cut off all contact with New Hope. And for Bud there is the freedom not to attend the presentation at all.

Before setting out on his venture, Bernie announces, *I feel solidarity with this group.* Benjamin says, *I support you.* Bernie says, *I want to go out and be able to interact with them, eat meals with them, and do whatever it takes to transcend the current setup*. Brenda says, *I'm with you,* and then adds, as if with some sense of what lies ahead, *so far.*

End Part I

Lessons

What am I seeing?

◊

Belief, knowledge, courage. The essential elements of system power are: the belief that power is a possibility for you, a deep understanding of system processes, and the courage to act. In essence this means the ability to recognize the System Story as it is happening, step out of the story, and create a new story. Early on I highlighted three New Hope members who would not be considered the central "power players" in this story, yet I believe their experiences are illuminating in this regard: Elite Edie, Middle Micky, and Immigrant Betsy. In one sense, everyone—with the possible exception of Bernie—is at this point caught up in the System Story, but I believe the costs are greater for these three members than for the others.

I see Edie caught up in a "directional differentiation" dilemma: Edie's core is submerged; she goes along with the dominant (Elizabeth's) direction, never fully at home with it, and behaving inconsistently, sometimes in accordance and sometimes in opposition.

I see Micky deep in the throes of "personal disintegration"; at times it's as if the person Micky, as an independent, thinking individual with a mind of his own, isn't present. He is in an unending game of Ping-Pong and he is the ball, battered to and fro.

I see Betsy submerged in the WE, regularly disagreeing with the thrust of the Immigrant group, regularly expressing her disagreement, being ignored, and still going along.

There is discomfort here for all three. So now the question is: What would happen if they (any one of them) (a) believed they had the power to change their condition in the system and the condition of the system, (b) had deep knowledge of the System Story and recognized how they were living it out, and (c) had the courage to step out of the story and create a new one?

Unfortunately, there is no predicting what form such actions would take or what consequences they would have. (Only the unhappy stories are predictable.) What you can do is put yourself in their positions. You now know the System Story, and you have a fairly good sense of life in New Hope. What would be the courageous act you would take if you were Edie or Micky or Betsy? How would your freedom act affect you? What consequences would it have for the system?

CHAPTER
8

Last Hope, Lost Hope: Part II

Last Hope 1

Bernie finds Elizabeth; he says he wants to speak with her before the Sharing of Visions meeting. Elizabeth agrees. Bernie's anger comes through. He tells Elizabeth, *You have no understanding of how the other side lives. You cannot even give me food. Who are you to have food to give me when I need it and don't have it? Who are you who can choose to be bountiful or not? This is a have/have not society only because the Elite are keeping it that way and the Elite can change it.*

Elizabeth's response is to tell Bernie the familiar story. *You were poor immigrants and we took you in. We have assets to share and there is work to be done...*

This infuriates Bernie; he cuts her off. *I have things too,* he says. *You're not the only one with assets. Screw your story. I'm not interested in integrating or in joining; I'm interested in something else...*

Well, that's your reality, says Elizabeth as she heads off for her meeting.

Two Societies

The presentations of the current realities of the two societies begins.

Brenda presents for the New Society. She is lively and enthusiastic; her love for the New Society shines through. She is proud of it, she sees it as a beautiful thing, and she has a high commitment to communicating her image clearly. She draws the New Society as an amoeba-like creature—composed of independent parts moving off in separate directions, yet remaining one unified creature. She lists the purposes of the New Society:

- to educate and learn from one another
- to share experiences
- to share resources—intellectual as well as material
- to appreciate solidarity and positive group feeling
- to accept and feel comfortable with the fact that some things (presumably integration) cannot work

She then presents the current realities of the New Society:

- We love one another.
- We don't care a rat's ass about what the other collection of people are doing.
- We are an open system; we welcome anyone to join us in what we do.
- Each of us is enabled to do our own thing, and we have support from the group to do it.

The presentation has great impact. Ernest and Edie are particularly moved...as is Micky. It is clear how different a reality this is from that of the Elite and Middles.

Elizabeth makes her presentation. The contrast is stark. She lists the purposes of New Hope:

- re-vision
- re-organization
- re-integration
- re-leasing of energy
- re-newal

She describes the current reality:

- We have a new structure.
- We have to maintain certain previous commitments to the principles and laws of New Hope.
- We are maintaining ourselves at a lower level of existence. She

explains, *We brought people here to work; that didn't work out, so we've had to hire outside help and use our resources.*

- We are unique individuals, working together, and we remain open to other people.

Elizabeth then presents the problems facing the New Hope Society, the last of which is: *We are a reality-based society. People are living in a building we own; there is no recognition of that; they are squatters. We don't want to evict people, but we do feel strongly about bringing people in and having them just use our property. We feel a need to negotiate the terms under which people are living there.*

At first there are no reactions. Maureen, who has been acting as moderator, asks, *What does the group need right now?* Benjamin says dismissively, *A stiff drink.*

But Micky has something to say: *I am envious. I see them as unified, a high esprit de corps, despite all that's happened. I have not been happy.*

Elizabeth comes in quickly, right on top of Micky's statement. *Are there any questions about anything I said?*

Micky's Continuing Dilemma

Micky and Mitch are talking in the kitchen of their cottage. Micky has a problem with Maureen. *She's eating our food, living in our home, and not paying for any of this. I have to account for rent and meals.* And there is more. *What will our role be tomorrow if there are no Immigrants to manage?* Mitch says that he is firmly aligned with New Hope, but Micky is not so sure. He has been struck by Brenda's presentation; the New Society has great appeal for him: to be free of these concerns about Maureen's rent and the role of Middles, and to be part of a community in which people care about one another.

Ernest and Edie Have Been Touched

The Elite are sharing their reactions to the presentations. Ernest and Edie had been moved to tears. *I felt very somber,* says Edie. Ernest agrees. *I cried because something real was happening,* he says. And to Elizabeth he says, *I feel that you are still in the role of the Elite, and I'm not sure I can go on with this.* Edie says, *They feel empathy with one another, and us, with all our trappings...*

Last Hope 2

Bernie finds the Elite and the Middles in the Elite cottage. He had looked in on Elizabeth's presentation and now dismisses it as *the same old story. I didn't get much out of it, and I doubt if the others in my group did, either.* Bernie says that the whole society is stuck. *It won't work if you try to join their new society...and they certainly are not going to join yours.* Bernie says he is interested in creating something new, *something greater than the other two societies. We could start from scratch...right now.*

Bernie is offering a third way—neither New Hope nor New, but something else that could be created afresh.

It is Elizabeth who speaks first. *How would I fit in?*

Bernie says that the society could begin with the two of them. *We, you and I, would get together; we could share our resources and start to build a society.* He asks Elizabeth, *Do you want to go ahead?*

This notion has some appeal to Maureen, who is now in limbo between the New Hope and New Societies. *I'm interested too,* she says, but she is ignored. This is between Bernie and Elizabeth.

Do you want to go ahead? Bernie asks.

Could it be on land that I own? says Elizabeth.

No, says Bernie.

It's one of the assets I own, says Elizabeth.

No, says Bernie.

I am willing to share the building and the floor and the heat. I own these, says Elizabeth.

Bernie: *I don't experience that you own these.*

Elizabeth: *I built it.*

Bernie: *You* say *you built it. But let's say that you do own this building; that's your resource, and I have my resources, too. Through my skills I have created access to the old country; I can have a car available to me within ten minutes; I have access to food, to a telephone.* (It is difficult for me to capture the full power of what is happening here; it goes beyond the dialogue. It is as if a different spirit has descended on the two of them. Elizabeth has been the most powerful of the Elite, the most committed to the legitimacy of the position, and to the history that justifies it. But now all of that is beginning to crumble, to be replaced by what? Something new? Nothing? Uncertainty? There is a dance that Elizabeth had danced with great elegance throughout, and now that dance is beginning to tremble.)

Elizabeth is drawn to this new possibility, but she has her reservations. *I'm not willing to share everything I have,* she says, *I want to keep my privacy, my living space. I want to continue living with the people I'm living with.*

That may be all right with me, says Bernie. *Not everything has to be equal.*

I could share some of my financial resources, says Elizabeth, *but I need to keep a nest egg...I feel I have worked very hard for what I have.*

How will they make decisions? Bernie suggests that they make a contract, that they operate by consensus. Elizabeth says, *I might be asked to give up everything I've worked for. I have a fear that at some point I'd be coerced into giving up things I don't want to give up.*

Bernie restates the contract. Consensus, agreement by both or a willingness to go along. *Does that give you enough control?*

Yes, says Elizabeth.

This Is a Good Group

While Bernie and Elizabeth have been exploring the possibility of creating a third way, the Immigrants have been meeting in their cottage. Much of the conversation is about THEM—how Mitch is hurting, how Edie showed no emotion at the presentation, how Edie needs everything in writing, how Edie flipped out over the Enablers coming in late, how the Elite haven't moved at all, how they lack sensitivity, how they take no action, how inept the Middles have been. Brother Bart says, *They've failed. You've got more life here.* And Bob agrees: *This is a good group.*

Regrets

Ernest and Edie have been off by themselves, talking together, crying together. Edie talks about the parallel she sees between her experience and Bernie's. *He felt his spirit alive at the outset, but denied it all the time just to stay loyal to his group.* She tells of a statement her grandfather used to make: *You cannot steer your ship by another man's compass.*

Last Hope 3

Bernie and Elizabeth continue their building process while Maureen, Mitch, and Micky observe. Bernie and Elizabeth appear stunned by what they have accomplished. For Elizabeth, there is a coming apart of the beliefs and history and story that have constituted her eliteness. All of that seems to have melted away. What remains is this intense and isolated relationship with Bernie, a sense of awe at this new coming together, along with confusion, vulnerability, and fear.

Bernie says that his stomach is in a knot. Elizabeth says, *I am amazed…stunned…overloaded. I have an enormous amount of regret. I see a thousand things I didn't see before, things I could have done. I see it in terms of all those people in your cottage. I see my own limitations.*

Bernie suggests that they continue making agreements with one another.

Elizabeth is thoughtful. *Do I now say that I give up my prior agreements?*

Bernie: *No, we didn't agree to that. Why do you ask?*

Elizabeth: *I agree to it.*

Bernie: *Are you comfortable with that agreement?*

Elizabeth: *Yes.*

For Bernie this is a major breakthrough. Elizabeth, the key Elite, now renounces the agreements she has made as an Elite. Surely this is an opening for a new beginning.

Bernie leaves; he is eager to share this development with the people in his cottage.

Someone Else Gives Up Prior Agreements

Micky has been observing the interaction between Elizabeth and Bernie. This last has special significance for him. He, too, has been burdened by the prior agreements he had made as a Middle in the New Hope Society. It is possible for him to give up his agreements. Micky also leaves, making his way to the New Society.

A Difference Too Great

Bernie returns to the New Society cottage. He talks of the new beginning he and Elizabeth have created and of the possibility of transcending the two current societies. There is an invitation in this but no apparent interest in accepting it. Bernie is treated as a joke; integration is his thing, it has nothing to do with them. The agreement that liberated the members of the New Society to pursue their individuality freed Bernie to undertake his new venture. But Bernie's difference seems to be too great for the New Society to tolerate. Bernie had the right to do his own thing, but he did not have the right to be taken seriously. After a few minutes of bantering, Bernie leaves.

Micky remains.

A Fading Glimmer of Interest

Micky is center stage in the New Society for quite a while. There is some effort to draw him into the anti-Elite spirit of the New Society, but Micky is not here out of antagonism toward the Elite. He talks about how different the Elite are when they're with the Middles. *They aren't somber then.* Micky tells the story of Bernie's building community. They are all stunned at how simple it was for him to break through to Elizabeth. Micky tells them about Ernest and Edie leaving the meeting in tears, saying that they were heartbroken. And Micky tells them that Bernie and Elizabeth have made certain agreements as to how they will live, interact, and deal with issues in their community.

There is a fleeting interest in this new development, a quick glimpse as to its possible significance. Betsy expresses interest in learning more. But the moment passes. The eating and drinking and light-hearted mood continue. And it is agreed that Micky will conduct a seminar tomorrow on bird-watching.

Politics and Last Hope

The process of community building continues. Maureen gets a glass of wine and joins Elizabeth and Bernie. She asks, *Does an opportunity exist to join your community?* Elizabeth asks Bernie, *What do you think?* Bernie asks Maureen if she agrees to operate by the fundamental principles: consensus, respect, sharing. Maureen says, *Yes, I do.*

But now something strange begins to happen. Only a symbolic gesture seems necessary for Maureen's induction into the new community: a nod, a handshake, a toast. But nothing comes. Elizabeth seems eager to accept Maureen, but Bernie is less eager to move ahead. He delays; he starts to present new principles, none of which are particularly clear; he suggests postponing dealing with Maureen's request until tomorrow. Elizabeth says she would like to deal with Maureen's request now. The atmosphere in the room has changed. Ernest senses it; he says to Bernie, *The impact you had thirty minutes ago was very powerful; the impact you have now is considerably less powerful.*

The difference between Bernie and Elizabeth at this moment is this: Elizabeth is not feeling political and Bernie is. Elizabeth is not concerned with the implications of specific actions for the total community; she is open. *I feel like sharing all now,* she says. But Bernie has other considerations. He has set out to demonstrate that it is possible "to transcend what is." He has already made major inroads to the people in this house: Elizabeth is in, Maureen is at the door, and, given their reactions, Ernest, Edie, and Mitch are not unlikely candidates. The problem is not in this house; it is in the house down the road.

Bernie has a vision that is both appealing to him and frightening. He sees this as the Big Move, the last hope of creating one community. He shares his vision with Elizabeth. He would invite the members of the New Society to sit around and observe while he and Elizabeth demonstrated how they work together as a new community. The others would watch...and join in if they chose. There is a big risk in this for Bernie. *How the others might react to this really frightens me,* he says.

Bernie continues to delay Maureen's entry. There is tension in the room; the magic spell has been broken. Edie and Ernest leave, and Elizabeth says, *Their leaving feels real scary for me.*

Maureen is at last accepted into the new community. Bernie shares his concern that the more successful he becomes in converting ex-Elite and ex-Middles, the more difficulty he may have with the ex-Immigrants. He needs to find some way to bring the others into the process. He asks Elizabeth and Maureen to wait while he goes back to check with the people he left behind.

Last Hope Becomes a Dirty Joke

Bernie enters the New Society cottage. Brother Bart is there, along with all the New Society members, including Micky. The atmosphere is loud and boisterous, with conversations going on all around the room.

Micky sees Bernie and shouts out to him, *Did you enroll any new members?*

Bernie says, *Yes, and I have important stuff to tell.*

He captures the attention of the Immigrants and then continues. *What I am up to is to break through all the crap...*really *break through. I did it, and I met with overwhelming success.*

There is snickering, but Bernie plows on. *I want to tell you about a new love, even as I have something going with the old.*

Bob shouts out, *I can't bear to tell you what usually happens in phases two and three of these things.* Lots of laughter. Bud calls out to Bernie, *You getting it off over there with her?*

Bernie sees the hopelessness of the situation. He says with some sarcasm, *I'm glad to see there's some interest in this.*

Bud replies, *Listen, if it makes you happy, that makes me happy.* Bernie leaves.

Brother Bart turns to the others and says, *Folks, you are so cynical. Let him enjoy his high. Just be there to pick up the pieces.*

The bantering continues. Betsy alone expresses her disappointment. She was interested in what happened over there, and was looking for more information. But she let the moment pass.

Epilogue

The following morning it was announced by the staff that the Society of New Hope experience was over. Saying it was over was one thing, having it really be over was quite another. There was a pre-breakfast meeting on the green, at which the staff described the new arrangements regarding housing, meals, and debriefing activities, which were to begin at 9:00 A.M. For the New Society, however, these new arrangements were not quite new enough. There were two major sticking points. The first had to do with the dining room. New seating arrangements did not change the fact that the dining room itself was not neutral territory. Since their independence, the New Society had established their cottage as their dining room; the conference center dining room was THEIR territory, New Hope territory. The second sticking point had to do with the very nature of the upcoming activity. All participants were to meet together, to look into one another's experiences over the past several days, and to use these interactions to deepen their understanding of social systems and power. That form of interaction itself was experienced—particularly by members of the New Society—as having political implications; it was "integration" in a form that the New Society had fought so strongly against.

Only with great reluctance did the members of the New Society move into the dining room, and once there, they chose to sit with one another rather than mix with THEM.

Over breakfast there is a discussion about what to do next. Bob says, *"Nothing's changed; it's just a change of accommodations. Let's not stop the society. Let's just invite them to our seminar."*

At 8:45, Edie, Elizabeth, and Ernest, Maureen, Micky, and Mitch leave the dining room and begin the move to the meeting room. The New Society members remain at their table, and their conversation continues.

At 9:00 Bernie gets up and goes to the meeting room, where the others are waiting.

End

Lessons

What am I seeing?

◊

And now we come to what is for me such a stunning paradox of system life. Standing outside of this story, I see it as a thing of beauty; yet on the inside, from the perspectives of the players, none of this beauty is apparent. Maureen, years later, when considering returning to New Hope, described this first experience as "ghastly." Ghastly! Maureen, how can you of all people feel this way? So many times you were our heroine—a force for independence, standing your ground, searching and sometimes finding that powerful third middle way. Don't you see the beauty in all this? The flowering of this society? How beautiful was the perfect dis-integration of the Middles. Mitch floating up to the Elite, Micky finding his home in the New Society, and you still searching for the third way…and coming so close.

And what about the unfolding story of the Immigrants—how could you fail to appreciate the beauty in that? How quickly that odd assortment of personalities jelled into so unified a WE. Bob, seeing violence everywhere and ever ready to return it; Brenda , the socialist (nothing less than full equality would satisfy her) and justified in her criminal behavior *(If they're dumb enough to leave the store unlocked)*; Benjamin, the patient negotiator maneuvering his way between a recalcitrant Elite and an equally recalcitrant Immigrant group; Bud, a hard worker among the slackers; Betsy, the enigma, always puzzled by the intensity of her group's anti-Elite stance, stuck in this group that provides nothing but safety for her, unwilling to confront or to leave. Under what conditions would such a diverse collection bond so tightly? "We're a good group," said Bob. And the Immigrants come together, feeling close to one another and separate from all the rest. "Why, we're almost communist," crowed Bernie.

And then at last the final separation; the New Society, they were our Basques, our Kurds, our Quebecois, separatists throughout history, seeking to get out from under the thumb of the dominant society. But it couldn't end there, could it? The dance within the dance. The uniformity was not perfect; it never is. So there was Bernie—our archetypal Bridge, breaking ranks; Hegel's man—thesis, antithesis, and Bernie searching for the new resolution, the synthesis. And he came so close.

So many graceful dances in one ballet. Edie and Benjamin in their pas de deux—Edie: "Let the terrorism end and then we will make peace"; Benjamin: "First make peace, then the terrorism will end." Dance that one again and again; dance it here in New Hope, dance it in Northern Ireland, dance it in Israel. As with all archetypal dances, we all know the steps.

And what of Elizabeth's journey? Queen. Guardian of the empire. Clever. Duplicitous. Yet, given the inevitable crumbling of the empire, did not she play her part perfectly? The jockeying, maneuvering, turning weakness into strength. Could Cardinal Richelieu have handled himself more adroitly? And then there is that dramatic coming apart. And you, Maureen, had the great good fortune to witness it. We talk about the great transformations, but how often do we see it? From order to disorder and then the emergence of a new order. Powerful stuff, played out right before your eyes. Ghastly?

And Edie, what she did for all of us. The remorse. The human tragedy known to so many of us—having lived one's life not at the direction of one's own inner voice, recognizing at the last gasp the loss of the road not taken. What do you think, Maureen, could she have found a compatriot in Immigrant Betsy? Do you suspect that she, too, had been carried away in other people's plans?

I ask you, Maureen, could Shakespeare himself have written a more striking drama?

This is the drama of the System Story, but what of the possibility of creating a new story?

Put yourself in Betsy's position in those last hours of New Hope. Both Micky and Bernie have described these amazing new developments going on in the cottage down the road. You are curious about this, interested. But once again you are alone in your interest. How are you feeling? What would you do?

I am sure that at this point Betsy sees herself as a minor player in New Hope. No power here. Who could care about her curiosity, her interest? So she says nothing and does nothing, and once again her moment passes. And as I write this I think about myself in "One That Got Away" (Part I, Chapter 3). There I was standing on the green as the Elite said, "We need Middles. Are there any volunteers?" And it never entered my mind that I could raise my hand and say, "I'll be your Middle." And so my moment passed. And I can't help but wonder what would have been, had Betsy seen her moment, risen, and said, "You know, folks, I really am curious about what is happening over there, and I'm going over to see." And away she goes. Suddenly I see a crack in the System Story and the possibility…only a possibility…of a new story emerging.

Part III

Seeing and Leading the Whole

CHAPTER
9

Exhilarating Concepts

When I was a student at the university, the course that thrilled me most was not psychology or sociology or philosophy, or any of the social sciences; it was Introductory Physiology—the workings of the human body. I remember the study method I often used, striding through my apartment, giving dramatic lectures to imaginary audiences, waxing enthusiastically over the elegance of the human body—so many distinct parts, so many different processes, each performing its function, yet all working together to produce one remarkable whole. At the time I took this enthusiasm as evidence of my fate as a physician. I was wrong; my fate was to be a systems thinker, and at the time I had no notion of what a systems thinker was.

My most profound experiences in New Hope came at those moments when I was struck with great clarity by the universality of the processes I was experiencing or observing. It was then that I experienced what I call *exhilarating concepts,* that is, concepts that illuminate processes at *all* levels of system life. Whichever way I looked, inward or outward, those same processes were operating; processes that were descriptive of New Hope were also descriptive of the functioning of the human body, of me (and you) as a person, of our organizations, religions, philosophies, nations, and so forth. Is there any significance to this other than the aesthetic nature of it all? I believe so. We will see how understanding these exhilarating concepts, and *seeing them as we are living them*, is essential to our creating sane and healthy social systems. And, conversely, we will see how blindness to these processes regularly leads the best of us into destructive nonsense.

Before getting into that, let me back up a bit to give you a better sense of my relationship to exhilarating concepts. Somewhere in my student readings I came across the distinction between *fate* and *potential*, not as they relate to human destiny but with regard to the life of a plant cell—for example, the life of a stem cell of a split-leaf philodendron. In the normal course of events this cell would spend its life as a stem cell; however, if the lead leaf of the plant is removed, that cell which was fated to be a stem cell reveals its potential and develops into a leaf cell. The potential was always there, but it was shut off. That basic life principle—*the potential was always there, but it was shut off*—resonated with me profoundly, and it continues to resonate with me. It manifests itself at all levels of system life. I remember my first crude application. When working with a group, there would usually be one or two people who dominated the early discussions. After a bit, I would ask these folks to pull back from the group and observe silently. Then others who had been silent would begin to speak, and after a bit I would pull them out. I would repeat this process until we were left with a handful (sometimes only one or two people) who had not yet spoken. Then they would begin. And theirs were often the deepest, richest, most thoughtful conversations. *The potential was always there, but it was shut off.* What thrills me about this simple concept is its universality, its functioning at all levels of systems from plant life to the human cell, right up to the functioning of social systems. We will be exploring the significance of this concept in our upcoming discussions of two universal system processes: differentiation and homogenization.

Concepts thrill me when they appear to reveal some fundamental truth of existence; it feels like coming as close as we mortals can to God's truth. Not only do they illuminate approximations of truth, but they also shed powerful light on human error.

In Part III I will ask you to explore with me three pairs of universal system processes:

- *autonomy and connectedness*—system parts (such as organs in the human body and members in social systems) have their independent lives, and they also function as components of an integrated whole (the body, group, team, organization, nation)
- *diversity and commonality*—systems as wholes differentiate, that is, they develop a variety of functions and processes that become increasingly different from one another, and these differentiated functions and processes maintain their commonality with one another
- *stability and change*—systems maintain continuity in form and function over time, and they change form and function over time

These processes are simple, and they are profound. They initially stemmed from my observations of New Hope. In time I began to see these processes operating at all levels of system life, from the human cell to the organization to all of humanity. A deep understanding of these processes is essential to system leadership, for they lie at the heart of whether our systems are healthy or unhealthy, functional or dysfunctional; whether we live in partnership with one another or are alienated from one another; whether our systems are stuck at mediocre levels of performance or rise to previously unimaginable levels of productivity and creativity; whether we humans live in peace and understanding with one another or fall into our historic patterns of domination, discrimination, oppression, and mutual destruction.

In the sections to follow we will explore various facets of these universal processes and their implications for system leadership. Following each section, you will find exercises and discussion questions aimed at helping you delve more deeply into these exhilarating concepts and explore their significance in relation to your own role as system member or leader. I encourage you to do more than simply read the exercises. I encourage you to *do* them; they are essential to getting to the heart of whole system understanding and leadership.

CHAPTER 10

Processes of the Whole: What Does IT Do?

IT:

INDIVIDUATES	and	**INTEGRATES**
DIFFERENTIATES	and	**HOMOGENIZES**
STABILIZES	and	**CHANGES**

What It Does

Three Pairs of Whole System Processes

Systems **INDIVIDUATE**

and they **INTEGRATE.**

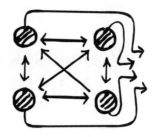

The members operate independently of one another...

and they interact with one another, functioning as components of an integrated whole.

Systems **DIFFERENTIATE**

and they **HOMOGENIZE.**

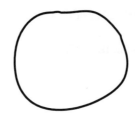

The whole develops variety (diversity) in form and function, with the forms and functions becoming increasingly different from one another...

and system knowledge and capacity are spread throughout the system so that these differentiated forms and functions maintain their commonality.

Systems **STABILIZE**

and they **CHANGE.**

Systems maintain continuity in form and function over time...

and they change form and function over time.

Some Clarifications

Between Individuation and Differentiation

INDIVIDUATION   **DIFFERENTIATION**

Differentiation is not about the number of people; it refers to the variety of processes, whether done by few or many members. For example:

- One person in a room might be a highly differentiated entity, performing many different functions: writing, finishing furniture, preparing dinner, making phone calls, balancing the checkbook.
- Fifty persons in a room might still be a relatively undifferentiated system if all of them are performing the same or similar functions—making phone calls, for example. (Clearly, fifty persons in a room could be a highly differentiated system if there are a variety of processes they are engaging in.)
- A highly individuated (and undifferentiated) basketball team would be one in which all the players were highly skilled offensive shooters with each operating independently of the others.
- A differentiated basketball team has a variety of processes: passing, shooting, and a vast repertoire of offensive and defensive plays.

Between Integration and Homogenization

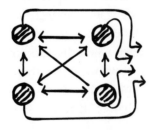

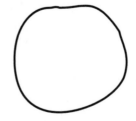

INTEGRATION   **HOMOGENIZATION**   **115**

- Homogenization is an experience of oneness: differences fade into the background, melt away, or are not present. Malcolm X described the homogenized experience of his hajj (religious pilgrimage to Mecca), in which all differences in color, race, nationality faded into the background. Many shared spiritual experiences are of this type.
- Integration has to do with oneness of function or mission, yet the components can be highly differentiated. Just as all the organs and processes of the body are quite different from one another, yet they coordinate with one another in the service of keeping us alive and functioning.
- At a sports event, good teams are highly integrated entities, the players feeding and supporting one another, and modulating their behavior in the service of the larger whole, the Team. But when a spectacular play occurs, thousands of fans in the stands—from all walks of life, and differing social classes, races, creeds, and colors—rise in excitement in a homogenized experience; at that moment the differences among them fade.

Contributions to System Health and Dysfunction

All six functions contribute to the health of the whole.

The system is enhanced when all members do their part (individuation), and it is weakened when they don't. The system is enhanced when all members work together in the service of the system as a whole (integration), and it is weakened when they don't.

The system is enhanced when it develops a variety of forms and functions enabling it to cope with the dangers in its environment and to prospect among the opportunities (differentiation), and it is weakened when it fails to develop this variety. The system is enhanced when system knowledge and capacity are diffused throughout the system so that members understand, respect, and can perform one another's functions and experience a oneness with each other (homogenization), and it is weakened when they do not.

The system is enhanced by maintaining continuity and stability over time (stabilization), and it is weakened when it doesn't. The system is enhanced when it is able to change in response to changing environmental conditions (change), and it is weakened when it does not.

Imbalance

Although system health requires all six processes, we shall see that for a variety of reasons, systems become imbalanced. As you read the following descriptions of imbalanced systems, see if they connect with systems in which you are a member.

Imbalanced Systems	Symptoms
Individuated, under-integrated	System members "do their own things"; concerted system efforts are weak, short-lived, or nonexistent; there is duplication, redundancy, missed opportunities for synergy; members compete with or are indifferent to one another's concerns.
Integrated, under-individuated	The focus is on the system's mission at the expense of the individual missions of its members; there are pressures to conform; members feel suppressed by the system; there is apathy; members feel that they are not using themselves fully, expressing their voices.
Differentiated, under-homogenized	The system is over-specialized; parts are out of touch with one another; there is little sense of commonality; there is much misunderstanding among system parts, leading to turf warfare, culture wars, gender battles, racial and ethnic strife.
Homogenized, under-differentiated	The system is too simple; it fails to take advantage of opportunities; it fails to protect itself against dangers; in its sameness, the system lacks richness; it is unstimulating for its members.

Stable, unchanging	The system is rigid; it continues to do what it has always done even when what it has always done is no longer relevant; it fails to take into account current realities; it fails to speak to the changing needs of its members and the changing conditions of its environment.
Changing, under-stabilized	The system is rootless; there is no enduring sense of mission or purpose; it floats from fad to fad; there is no history or accumulated wisdom to draw from; the system is sterile with no rites, rituals, holidays, celebrations.

Lesson 1:

Discussion Questions

Use these questions as a guide to begin working with these concepts in your life.

1.   Choose three different systems in which you are leader or a member. (These might include your family, your work group, your organization, the country, your school or college.) Analyze each of these in terms of balance. Where systems are in imbalance, consider the consequences that imbalance has for you, other members, and the system as a whole.

2.   Examine the tensions in society regarding race, gender, and sexual orientation from the framework of these system processes. In doing so, think of the whole of society as the system, and race, gender, and sexual orientation as differentiations of the whole.

3. New position for you: Homogenizer. Think of some system you
are connected with that is suffering the negative consequences of
over-differentiation. Is it your manufacturing or service organization?
Your religious affiliation? Your health-care system? Your family? Your
college or university faculty? Your college campus with differentiated
housing and curricula based on race, gender, or sexual orientation? Be
clear about what the costs of over-differentiation are to you, to the
system's members, and to the system as a whole. You have been
hired as a Homogenizer (a brand new twenty-first century role). Your
job is to bring homogenization into that system without destroying
the positive consequences of differentiation. (1) What is your overall
strategy? (2) What specific actions will you take, or what processes
will you put in place? (3) How do you plan to deal with the resistance
you are likely to encounter? (4) How do you like this new position?

CHAPTER

11

Politics and Preferences

There are people who don't like the stories I told in Part I. For some it is a matter of discomfort; these are not actions they would be comfortable in taking, nor are they comfortable having people take these actions around them. But for others, their judgments are based on something other than comfort; they see such actions as wrong. *This is more of that worn-out white male, patriarchal, cowboy, western, Newtonian, competitive...etc. behavior.*

I confess to a bias: I am personally imbalanced (high individuation, low integration); I do my best work alone, I am comfortable with unilateral action, I often feel constrained in group settings. I bring this bias with me; it is clearly reflected in the stories in Part I. I do not, however, consider that bias a weakness to be overcome or an archaic relic to be transcended. It is my strength, and in it lies one of my unique contributions. Yet I recognize that it is also my vulnerability; how much more I could accomplish if only there were more Integrator in me. (In "Begging with Barry" I did demonstrate that when integration was called for, I could do the job, but that is not always the case.)

My point is: individuation and integration are often politicized. We extol the virtues of one process and demonize the other. In this politicized context, patriarchy and matriarchy are not theories, they are political parties. If I am an Integrator by nature, then I may feel overrun, abandoned, and disregarded in a setting in which Individuation is the prevailing culture—just as the Individuator is likely to feel constrained and stifled in settings in which integration is the prevailing mode.

Individuation and integration are neutral system processes; they both have powerful contributions to make to system health; and our systems are weakened when we suppress one process or the other.

We would do well to be equally cautious regarding the politicization of change and stabilization. In this "modern" world, if you value organizational stability, loyalty, and mutual responsibility among stockholders, management, and workers, you run the risk of being seen as *out of touch with the 21st century, stuck in the past. Get with the future!* and so forth.

Our challenge as system leaders and members is not to dismiss one another on political or any other grounds, but to recognize, value, support, and develop both of these orientations—individuation *and* integration; change *and* stabilization—in our systems.

In what follows, I describe the extremes in personal preference regarding individuation and integration, differentiation and homogenization, stabilization and change. It will be useful for you to be clear about where you stand on these processes.

Individuators *or*	**Integrators**
Individualists, loners, free marketeers, competitors; Individuators feel constrained by the group; they do their best work alone. They feel that too much integration deprives them of freedom, that it stifles individualism, entrepreneurism; they believe that the best results are produced by turning people loose.	Team players, cooperators, socialists; Integrators are energized by the group interaction; they work less well alone; they feel that the best work comes from group interaction. They feel that too much individuation breeds destructive competition, winners and losers, selfishness and greed.

Differentiators   *or*   Homogenizers

Differentiators prefer being with their own kind. (Their own kind might be their professional colleagues or their racial, religious, gender, or sexual preference group.) They are comfortable with their own kind; they understand one another easily; being with their own kind allows them to deepen important parts of themselves. They see homogenization as watering things down, taking the richness away.

Homogenizers are uncomfortable with difference; they see difference as divisive and destructive. They point to humankind's history of racial and ethnic warfare, current culture wars, and the destructive turf and territorial battles in our organizations and institutions. Homogenizers seek to tear down barriers and to focus on our commonalities rather than our differences.

Stabilizers   *or*   Changers

Stabilizers are conservative. They are comfortable with what is, and are reluctant to change. They tend to resist new fashions in clothes, hairstyles, cuisines, and so forth. They tend to stick to the old-time religion. They see Changers as faddist, as blowing with the wind, as lacking substance and depth.

Changers are perpetual modernists; they are attracted to what is new, whether in clothing styles, latest theories about organizational change, cuisine, architecture, art, dance steps, entertainment, hairstyles. They see Stabilizers as stuck in the past, blockers, resisters, anchors on development.

Lesson 2:

Discussion Questions

◊

Use the following discussion questions and exercises to explore the implications of preferences and politics for system leadership.

1. *Where are you on the Individuator-Integrator continuum?* Visualize (or draw) a continuum from Extreme Individuator (strong preference for working alone, feel uncomfortable or constrained in groups) to Extreme Integrator (strong preference as team player, most comfortable and most effective working in groups). Where do you place yourself on this continuum? If you are in a supervisory, management, leadership, or staff position, be sure that you place yourself on the basis of personal inclination and not on the basis of how you feel you must work, given your position.

2. *Where are you on the Differentiator-Homogenizer continuum?* Do the same for the continuum between Extreme Differentiator (strong preference for immersion in one's own specialty—or ethnic/racial/gender—group; is uncomfortable and feels diverted by homogenizing activities) and Extreme Homogenizer (strong preference for interdisciplinary—professional or cultural—activities).

Reflect on how your personal preferences can influence your role as system member or leader—the choices you make, which processes you support, and which you ignore or suppress.

3. *Group activity.* If you are working with all or some members of a system, have these members form a continuum around the room from Extreme Individuator (strong preference for working alone, feel uncomfortable or constrained in groups) to Extreme Integrator (strong preference as team player, most comfortable and most effective working in groups). If you have people who are in supervisory,

management, or leadership positions, be sure that they choose on the basis of personal inclination and not on the basis of how they feel they must work, given their positions. While people are still standing, have them talk about why they have placed themselves where they are.

Repeat this activity using the continuum Extreme Differentiator (strong preference for immersion in one's own specialty—or ethnic/racial/gender—group; is uncomfortable and feels diverted by homogenizing activities) to Extreme Homogenizer (strong preference for interdisciplinary—professional or cultural—activities).

Then have a conversation about how personal preference can influence our roles as system members and leaders—the choices we make, which processes we support, and which we ignore or suppress.

4.   *Group activity.* Have system members divide themselves into either Changers or Stabilizers. (Some people will have difficulty making the choice; acknowledge their dilemma but insist on their making a choice. Given their ambivalence, which orientation comes closest to describing them?) Give the Changers and Stabilizers ten minutes to deal with the following question: "What is the contribution your orientation (Change or Stabilization) makes to the life of this system?"

After ten minutes have each group present its position while the others simply listen without comment. Then give each group ten minutes to answer the following two questions. It is important that they answer both parts: "What is it about the other's orientation that causes you difficulty? Be specific." And "What is the value you derive from that orientation? Again, be specific."

Then sit together and have a conversation about that activity.

C H A P T E R
12

Systemic Imbalance

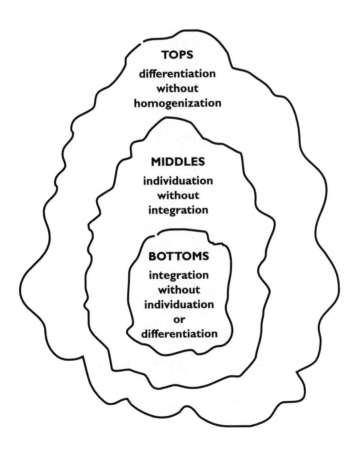

Nowadays in the Power Lab we have a differentiated staff of coaches and anthropologists. Coaches work with participants helping them see choices, think strategically, stretch their personal envelopes, and so forth. During New Hope, anthropologists are silent; they make no interventions; they merely observe and record.

In the early days there were no coaches, so we anthropologists, although silent for the most part, might make an occasional intervention. Most often I intervened no more than three times in each program, once for the Elite, once for the Middles, and once for the Immigrants. And in every case, the intervention focused on systemic imbalance.

Here we are going to revisit the System Story (Part II, Chapter 6) and examine Top, Middle, and Bottom positions against the framework of the three pairs of fundamental system processes. Again, our interest extends beyond New Hope to the other organizations and systems of our lives. (It might be useful for you to revisit the chart on page 58, which describes a range of familiar Top, Middle, and Bottom settings.)

Imbalance at the Top: Differentiation without Homogenization

Tops exist in a world of complexity and responsibility—lots of input to deal with, input from within the system and from the environment, difficult input, unpredictable input—and, collectively, Tops are responsible for the whole system.

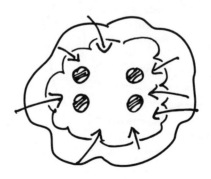

To cope with those conditions, the Top system differentiates; responsibility is divided, with each Top becoming responsible for some piece of the whole.

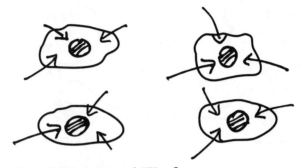

Turf and Directional Warfare

Differentiation often occurs without corresponding attention to homogenization. The consequence for Tops is that each becomes increasingly knowledgeable about and responsible for his or her own arena and decreasingly knowledgeable about and responsible for the arenas of other Tops. The Top system becomes increasingly territorial and vulnerable to destructive turf warfare:

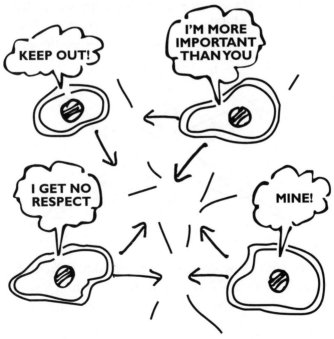

and to directional warfare:

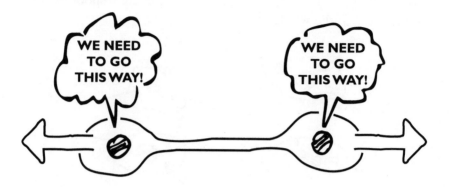

Imbalance in the Middle: Individuation without Integration

Middles exist in a tearing world—one that pulls them apart from one another, pulls them between demands from above and demands from below, and pulls them toward customers and toward suppliers. (One factor that differentiates the Middle and Top worlds is that Middles have their individual areas of responsibility and are not collectively responsible for anything.)

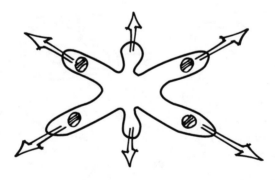

To cope with these conditions, the Middle system individuates. Individuation tends to be low-grade, with individual Middles operating independently of one another, not necessarily using themselves fully, not necessarily bringing to bear their unique skills and abilities, stretching, growing, and so forth.

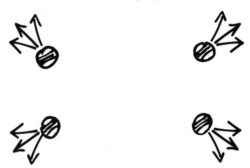

Isolation and Alienation

Individuation generally occurs without corresponding attention to integration. The consequence for Middles is that each Middle experiences the tearing alone; there is no Middle support system: Middles tend to be weak, confused; there is no Middle system with its unique perspective, function, or mission; and the potential contributions of Middles to system survival and development are unrealized.

Imbalance in the Bottom World: Integration without Individuation or Differentiation

Bottoms exist in a world of shared vulnerability, a world in which they feel endangered by some external force: top management, who at any moment might sell the company, shut a plant down, reorganize, change health-care plans, cancel an initiative and launch a new one; or by some foreign enemy; or by developers coming in to upgrade a poor or working-class neighborhood.

To cope with this vulnerability, the Bottom system integrates—the system coalesces; members feel closely connected with one another; a We-versus-Them mentality develops.

Groupthink

Integration generally occurs without corresponding attention to individuation and differentiation. There are pressures to remain unified. Individual members, not wanting to distance themselves from the group, conform to the group. Group members, uncomfortable with deviancy (fearing it will destroy unity), pressure others to conform. Differing strategies are experienced as potentially destructive. The Bottom system falls into groupthink: coercing deviants into line through force, love, education; exiling, hospitalizing, jailing, or murdering deviants when coercion fails; having debilitating internal struggles over which is *the* correct path to pursue.

In Search of Balance

Top, Middle, and Bottom systems need to adapt to their unique environmental conditions. It is functional for Tops to differentiate; otherwise they could easily be overwhelmed by unmanageable complexity. It is functional for Middles to individuate in order to lead, manage, or service the units they are supposed to lead, manage, or service. And it is functional for Bottoms to integrate as a protection against their vulnerability. *The challenge for all three systems is to adapt without falling into imbalance.*

In order to avoid turf and directional warfare, Tops need to balance differentiation with concrete homogenization strategies. In order to avoid isolation and alienation, Middles need to balance individuation with concrete integration strategies. And in order to avoid groupthink, Bottoms need to balance integration with concrete individuation and differentiation strategies.

Strategic and Emotional Considerations

Let us assume that each of these systems—Top, Middle, and Bottom—is striving for balance; in essence each would be attempting to become a system that is individuated and integrated, differentiated and homogenized.[1] But each, given its systemic condition, has unique challenges. One can develop a set of concrete strategies or agendas that would bring each system into balance. For example,

Homogenization and Integration Strategies for Tops

- *interchangeability.* Walking in one another's shoes. Spending time performing one another's functions, directly experiencing one another's worlds.
- *sharing high-quality information,* so that Tops are well aware of one another's conditions, dilemmas, issues, and so forth.
- *mutual coaching.* Using Top meetings for mutual coaching, which requires Tops to be open about the issues they are facing and to be open to being coached by their peers; it also requires Tops to be committed coaches to their peers.
- *a powerful shared vision.* Tops need to develop a powerful shared vision for the system they are collectively leading. *What are we jointly committed to?* This is critical because when directional differentiations arise, as they are likely to, it will be important for Tops to refocus on their shared vision. (By the way, if Tops cannot come up with a powerful shared vision of the system—whether these Tops be top executives, business partners, or couples in the family—this is a good indication that they ought not to become a Top system.)

Those of you who are in Top systems marked by turf warfare, or who work with such systems, may by now be rolling your eyes. *You're dreaming, Barry; there is no way these Tops are going to do any of these strategies. They are not going to open themselves to one another; they are not going to reveal their vulnerabilities; they are going to be very selective about the information they reveal; and, frankly, they are not going to be committed to one another's success.* And you are absolutely right. There are emotional considerations to deal with, and if these are not dealt with, all of our brilliant strategies, all of the lists of specific how-to's so many yearn for, will count for naught. As they often do. But let's continue with the strategies because they are important—though not sufficient—and then return to the emotional considerations.

Integration and Homogenization Strategies for Middles

- *a powerful shared vision.* This is even more difficult for Middles than it is for Tops. Tops are supposed to be jointly responsible for the whole; it is reasonable to expect them to have a shared vision. But Middle peers generally have no collective responsibility; each is only responsible for his or her own bailiwick. To build a powerful Middle system, however, it is critical that the Middles have a collective mission for themselves that is different from their individual missions and that contributes to the overall system mission. And the more challenging the mission, the better. *What is missing in this system? What can we Middles do that has never been done before? What can we accomplish better than it has ever been accomplished?*
- *a sacred commitment to regular meetings.* Such meetings are for Middle peers only, no Tops. Regular meetings are particularly difficult in the middle space, because it is the nature of that space to pull Middles away from one another and out toward those individuals and groups they manage, service, or coach.
- *integrative activities.* Some of the activities Middles would engage in during their regular meetings with one another are: sharing information, using that information to diagnose

systemwide conditions, problem solving, sharing best practices, mutual coaching, smoothing out or regularizing conditions across the system.

Once again you might say, *Nice list, Barry, but it won't work with my Middles. They (we) feel they (we) have little in common; they (we) are competitive with one another; they (we) are evaluative of one another; they (we) don't get along; they (we) don't believe there's any collective power in here. So why on earth would they (we) ever want to get together?* And once again, you are right; these are great strategies, but unless emotional considerations are dealt with, these strategies will never get off the drawing board.

Individuation and Differentiation Strategies for Bottoms

I'm assuming that the Bottom group already has some mission related to its vulnerability to Them—for example, to ward off the developers, to gain equitable treatment in the organization, to reverse some detrimental policy, to fight against oppression, to preserve their ethnic identity, and so forth.

- *encourage individual differences.* The Bottom system is composed of individuals with different skills, abilities, interests. Encourage members to use (risk) their uniquenesses *in the service of the system's mission.* The last phrase is key; this is not just about people going off and "doing their own thing," it is about encouraging individual differences but always in the service of the system's mission.
- *pursue diverse strategies.* Don't limit yourself to a single strategy, no matter how right that strategy feels. Come at your goal from a variety of directions—soft and hard, straitlaced and zany, rational and intuitive.

Again, there are reasons why such a logical set of strategies will not be accepted. In the Bottom space, individual actions and diverse strategies often feel threatening, divisive. *Straighten out, Barry, everyone knows that in unity there is strength; we hang together or we hang alone; united we stand, divided we fall...and so forth. All that individuality and diversity is heresy. You don't encourage that, you snuff it out.*

Once again it is clear, the emotional considerations must be dealt with.

Belief, Powerful System Knowledge, and the Courage to Act

If concrete strategies and specific how-to's were all we needed for system sanity, then the last book on leadership would have been written long ago. We have been deluged with good advice, yet the same problems keep recurring. To overcome the emotional considerations, we come back to our essential ingredients for system leadership:

Belief. All system members—Top, Middle, or Bottom—need to believe that power is a real possibility for their system. Top and Bottom systems are more likely to believe that they have the potential for power, however frustrated they are in realizing it. In Middle systems the belief that Middles have collective power is more difficult to come by.

Powerful system knowledge. Tops, Middles, and Bottoms need powerful system knowledge; they need to understand the System Story as they are living it; they need to understand the conditions their systems are in and how those conditions affect their relationships with one another; they need to know that their issues are systemic, not personal; they need to know that their challenge is not to fight, control, protect against one another, but to learn how to work together to master the space they are in. They need to develop this knowledge through reading, through coaching, through participation in experiential exercises, through discussion of systemic concepts. It is only against the background of this powerful system knowledge that the above strategies begin to make sense.

Courage. And ultimately it comes down to the courage to act. Now that we Tops know that these homogenizing and integrating strategies make sense for us, are we willing to let go of the past, our history, and momentum, and risk these new ways of relating? Now that we Middles understand that our powerlessness and alienation from one another are systemic, are we willing to step up to the challenges of finding a powerful mission for ourselves and integrating regularly with one another? Are we Bottoms willing to risk individuality and diversity? We know what our current stands produce: one variation or another of the System Story. Are we willing to step out of that story and create a new one?

Lesson 3:

Exercise

◊

Consider the following descriptions of system conditions. Choose the one that comes closest to a condition you are currently in. Then work with the exercises that follow.

A.   You are a member in a Top system (business partners, couple in the family, executive team) that is experiencing some of the turf and directional warfare issues described above.

B.   You are in a Middle system (peer middle managers, department heads, staff specialists, consultant group) that is experiencing some of the isolation and alienation issues described above.

C.   You are in a Bottom system (activist social action or neighborhood group, disgruntled employees, teachers, professors, physicians in a large managed-care system) that is experiencing some of the groupthink issues described above.

1.   Get crystal clear about what the power of your system *could* be if it were balanced. (If your Top system developed homogenization and integration processes. If your Middle system developed integration and homogenization processes. If your Bottom system developed individuation and differentiation processes.)

- What would you be able to accomplish that you are not able to accomplish now? And what would the system be able to accomplish?

- How would your feelings and the feelings of other system members change?

- How would your relationship with system members and their relationships with one another change?

There is no point in proceeding unless you can develop some excitement about the productive possibilities of balance for your system. The question is: Do you believe in the possibility of power for that system?

2.   At this point, you might be feeling what I was feeling just before I took action in the cases in Part I. You are uncomfortable with conditions as they are; you have a vision of what else your system might become; you have powerful knowledge related to your system's condition; you think (but are not positive) that you could make a difference. What strategies are beginning to emerge as to how you might begin to work with other members of your system? Notice how you are feeling as these strategies begin to take form. What are the risks you envision in moving ahead?

3.   So now, what are you going to do?

CHAPTER
13

High-Octane System Processes and the Challenge of Robust Systems

Albert Einstein said that science can only tell us what is. What could be *lies in the province of religion.*

Once we see system processes as they are, this opens up for us the possibility of what else they might be. There is the distinction between passively falling into a process and zestfully pursuing that process in depth. For example, when we spoke of systemic imbalance (Part 3, Chapter 12), we saw how Middle systems fall into individuation in response to the tearing conditions of their environments. This is often a low-grade form of individuation—*I go my way, you go yours.* But what exactly is *my* way—my uniqueness, talents, skills, interests, calling; and am I willing to find my way, and go my way—investing in it, developing it, using it fully, risking failure? Clearly this is a different order of individuation, one I am calling *high-octane individuation*.

Likewise, we find Top systems falling into differentiation in response to the conditions of their environments, and Bottom systems falling into integration in response to theirs. Again we ask the question: What possibilities open up for us and our systems as we move from processes that are simply pulled from us to processes we pursue actively, zestfully, and in depth?

And what are the possibilities of creating robust human systems, systems that develop far beyond balance, systems that take us to the edge of what is possible for us as human beings, systems that are:

zestfully individuated *and* zestfully integrated,

zestfully differentiated *and* zestfully homogenized,

zestfully stabilized *and* zestfully changing?

High-Octane Individuation

System members use themselves fully; they bring their unique skills and abilities—their specialness—to the system. They put themselves at risk—stretching, growing, learning.

High-Octane Integration

The system has a mission that inspires system members, that gives them a larger sense of purpose; members are fully committed to the system's mission; they modulate their own behaviors and zestfully support one another in the service of the system's mission.

High-Octane Differentiation

The system zestfully pursues its differences; there are varied spaces and functions in which people can sharpen their skills, deepen their interests, pursue their intellectual, emotional, physical, and spiritual questions. At the level of task, the system has many strategies for elaborating its mission, and it can flexibly re-differentiate (develop new strategies) in response to changing environmental conditions—new dangers to protect against, new opportunities to grasp.

High-Octane Homogenization

System members actively build bridges for mutual understanding. They develop processes for sharing knowledge and capacity throughout the system. They work at understanding one another's functions, conditions, experiences, and beliefs.

High-Octane Stabilization	**High-Octane Change**
The system has a history to which members are attached and that enriches their lives; it has an identity and continuing core purpose, which members are proud of; there is accumulated wisdom, which members draw upon, and rituals and celebrations, which add meaning to members' existence. The system builds on its past; it deepens itself.	The system is an active learner; it takes in information from its environment; it changes form and function in response to changing environmental conditions in order to protect itself from danger and to prospect among opportunities.

Lesson 5:

Discussion Questions and Activities

◊

1. *How robustly individuated are you?* Think about some system you care about—your family, work group, church, volunteer group, neighborhood. How robustly individuated are you in that system? What would high-octane individuation be for you? What are your unique skills and abilities, and are you using these fully in the service of the system? Are you stretching, growing, putting yourself at risk? What keeps you (and others) from robustly individuating?

2. *How robustly integrated is your system?* Think about some system in which you are a member and that you care about. Visualize that system's living a high-octane mission: to be something special in the world, to do something that has never been done before, to do something better than it has ever been done before.

3. *How robustly differentiated is your system?* Think of some path you might pursue in the service of the system's mission, a direction the system is not currently taking. (You need not follow this path alone; other system members may be joining you.) Visualize your system's following other richly varied paths in living its mission. How would all this differentiation change your life in the system? How would it change the system?

4. *Robust homogenization.* If you are successful in creating a robustly differentiated system, then you will need to develop equally robust homogenization processes by which all system members feel a part of all these varied strategies.

The history of our Power Lab staff may be informative in this regard. In the early days we were an undifferentiated staff; then we differentiated into anthropologists and coaches, each with contributory functions to our overall mission; over time we became increasingly specialized, increasingly expert in our specializations, and increasingly separate from one another. Then tensions—and some animosities—developed. It was clear that we were suffering the pains of high-octane differentiation without corresponding attention to homogenization and integration, so we developed processes for remedying the situation: interchangeability (rotating roles), daily all-staff meetings in addition to the separate meetings, and involvement of anthropologists in what had previously been exclusively coach roles.

Visualize processes your system is pursuing such that all members feel a part of all that is happening. How would these processes change your life in the system? How would they change the system?

5. *How robustly stabilized is your system?* What is it about this system that you deeply care about? What is it that you don't want to lose? What are its core principles? Get crystal clear about all the things that you cherish about this system. Take your time with this.

Do you celebrate the system's accomplishments?

Do you have rituals that lend meaning to your system life?

Do you break bread together?

Do your record and periodically review your history?

What else could you do?

6.   *How robustly changing is your system?* What is happening in your system's environment or in the world that is calling for the system to change? Are you actively tuning in to the environment? What is changing there? What new dangers are present? What new opportunities? Are you tuning in to systems similar to yours, studying how they are coping and prospecting in the environment? Is learning about the world in which your system functions a high priority of your system? Are you open to reinventing your system?

7.   *Visualize your system as a robust human system* characterized by all the processes you have described above. It is:

robustly individuated **and** robustly integrated,

robustly differentiated **and** robustly homogenized,

robustly stabilized **and** robustly changing.

How would such a system change your life? The lives of other system members? The world in which your system exists?

What would you and other system members need to give up in order to create such a system?

8.   *Creating a robust human system.* Are you committed to creating a robust human system? Do you believe it is possible?

You now have deep knowledge about the essential robust system processes: high-octane individuation, integration, differentiation, homogenization, stabilization, and change.

You also have deep knowledge about the pitfalls on the road to robustness: the limitations imposed by politics and preferences, the pull of environmental forces, the absence of courage.

Are you ready to take the next step: to involve system members in exploration of the above questions?

Part IV

*Lessons
from and for
the Cosmos*

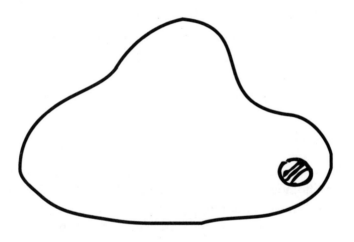

CHAPTER
14

System Story II: Righteous Warfare between Culture and Counterculture

It is difficult to see the System Story when we are living it; and that blindness has exacted a terrible toll on humankind. And the point is: We are always living one System Story or another.

Early on in the Power Lab I observed that no system remains homogeneous for very long. If an Elite (Top) system has a hard-line orientation, you can count on the eventual emergence of a soft-line counterculture within that Top system. If the Immigrant (Bottom) system is basically nonconfrontational, you can count on the emergence within the Bottom system of a confrontational counterculture. (Middle systems rarely develop a homogeneous orientation from which to diverge.) From the outside one might view these developments as aesthetically pleasing: the systems are expressing their possibilities, imbalanced systems are self-correcting toward balance. From the inside, however, the experiences are hardly aesthetic. Culture and counterculture experience one another as opponents, sometimes as bitter enemies.

The story of righteous warfare between culture and counter-culture is not limited to New Hope; it is played out in many forms—religious factionalism, culture wars, cold wars, hot wars—with all sides firmly entrenched in the righteousness of their position.

Political leaders—whether of the culture or counterculture—rally support, and sometimes lead their minions to battles of words or arms, by extolling the virtues of their position while demonizing the position of their opposite. System leaders, on the other hand, having a deep understanding of the dynamics of culture/counterculture, are faced with a more complex challenge. What follows is deep knowledge regarding culture/counterculture.

Just as there is a Top/Middle/Bottom System Story (Part II, Chapter 6), so is there also a Culture/Counterculture Story, variations of which are played out in many different arenas. The Culture/Counterculture Story is described below in the following section.

The Phases of System Life
Phase 1: Systems Face Choices

System members and leaders are faced with choices regarding the fundamental form their systems should take. The question is: Which form will best serve the system's ability to survive and thrive in its environment? Three choices revolve around the universal system processes as described in Part III.

Individuated System or Integrated System?

Should the system be a collection of independent individuals, with each member free to pursue his or her personal path; or should it be an integrated entity with members beholden to one another and to the system? How will system survival best be served? By turning members loose and allowing them to compete freely? Or by organizing them such that they feed and support one another and modulate their behavior in the service of the system's mission?

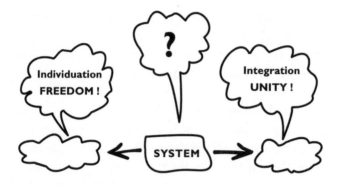

Differentiated System or Homogeneous System?

Should the system elaborate its differences and be enriched by them; or should it elaborate and focus on the commonality among system parts?

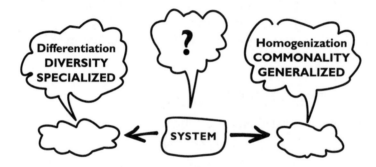

Stable System or Changing System?

Should the system remain constant over time, maintaining its traditions, forms, and processes; or should it regularly seek new and improved forms and processes?

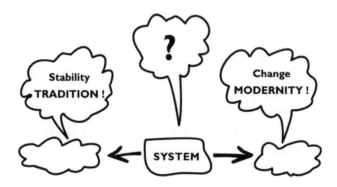

Phase 2: Systems Choose, and Their Choices Become Politicized

Systems choose; that is, they organize themselves around one pole or the other: they become primarily individuated (free) *or* integrated (unified), differentiated (diverse, specialized) *or* homogeneous (uniform), stable (traditional) *or* changing (modern). System leaders and members tend to politicize their choices; whichever pole the system chooses becomes the right choice, the only choice. They exaggerate the benefits of their system's choice while demonizing its opposite number.

So, for example, we see the political tension between the free society and the unified society.

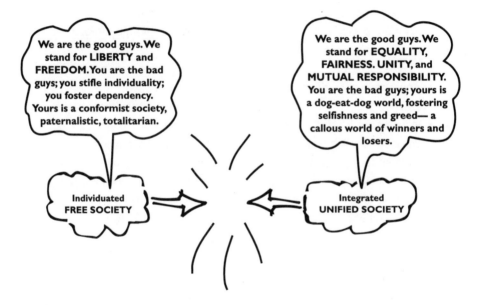

Phase 3: Pure Systems Decay

Politicization leads some system members to attempt to purify the system, to drive out all signs of its opposite process. For example, if our mission is to be a unified system, then we must drive out all the corrupting influences of freedom. Or, if our mission is to be an individuated system, then we must eliminate the corrosive forces of integration. Whatever faults the system has are attributed to the corrupting influences of its opposite process, or to the lack of zeal in pursuing its own basic choice.

As systems move toward becoming pure forms, the limitations of purity emerge; the system falls out of balance and begins to weaken. The system becomes less functional in its environment and less attractive to its members.

So, we see the signs of trouble and eventual decay as for example, individuated and integrated systems move toward purity.

Pure Individuation	Pure Integration
■ Relatively permanent class differences emerge. The rich get richer, the poor get poorer. The powerful get more powerful, the powerless remain powerless.	■ Diminished member initiative. (The system will take care of us, whatever we do.)
■ Class warfare.	■ Members feel suppressed, stifled, yearning to be free.
■ Anger among the poor and powerless.	■ Anger at the system because of its restraints.
■ Winners are focused on self-enhancement and have little commitment to the system.	■ Diminished commitment to the system's goals.
■ Losers feel betrayed by the system and have little commitment to it.	■ Increased actions aimed at subverting the system.
■ The fabric of community tears apart.	■ Diminished innovation regarding the system's goals; increased innovation regarding subversion.
■ There is danger of system upheaval—strikes, revolutions.	

Phase 4: The Emergence of Countercultures

As systems move toward purity, there emerges within them an opposing counterculture. The counterculture represents the initially rejected choice. The counterculture attacks the predominant culture for its failings while pointing to the virtues of its own culture. So, for example, in the individuated system there emerges an integrating counterculture.

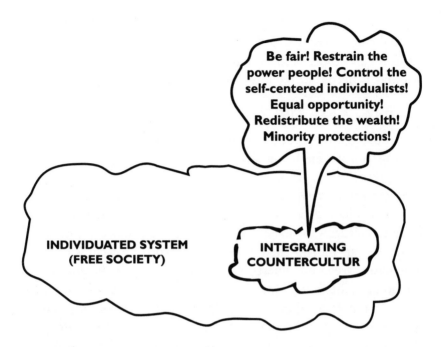

And in the integrated system there emerges an individuating counterculture.

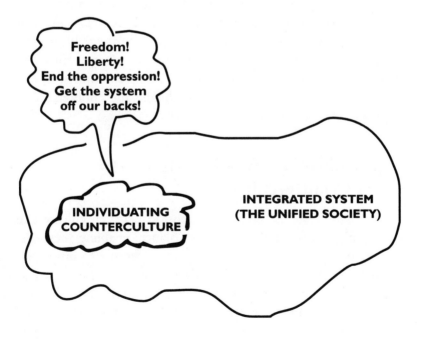

People who are viewed as traitors by members of the integrated culture are seen as heroes by members of the individuated culture, and those seen as traitors in the individuated culture are viewed as heroes in the integrated culture.

Phase 5: An Uneasy Balance

Although the counterculture is regularly attacked by the prevailing culture for being wrongheaded, heretical, or traitorous, *the prevailing culture is often saved from self-destruction by incorporating elements of the counterculture.* Each system preserves its ideology by continuing to demean the principles of the counterculture. So, for example, the United States prides itself on being an individuated system—extolling the virtues of individualism, freedom, liberty, free markets, and so forth—and it demonizes integrated systems (communism, socialism) for their suppression of freedom. Yet the United States, in order to avoid potential collapse through rioting, class and racial warfare, and revolution, has a history of incorporating many elements of the integrating counterculture: labor laws, Social Security, health and safety regulations, minimum wage, civil rights legislation, graduated income tax. Although one can make the case that the stability of the individuated system depends on its being balanced by these elements of the integrating counterculture, this does not stop the champions of individuation from continuing to demean the counterculture—as socialists, communists, threats to the vitality of the system—and to blame the counterculture for whatever weakness the individuated system has.

The Costs of Suppressing the Counterculture

For many systems the internal tension between culture and counterculture results in a workable balance, enabling these systems to survive. Other systems, in their pursuit of purity, self-destruct. For example, one could make the case that the collapse of the Soviet Union stemmed from its unrelenting drive for purity and its complete suppression of the counterculture. As a consequence, the system crushed the initiative of much of its population, and stifled the entrepreneurism and innovation needed to create a vital economy, while at the same time creating mounting pressures for freedom.

Systems can just as easily self-destruct by crushing the integrating counterculture. For example, for many people the collapse of the Soviet Union sounded the death knell for integration as a guiding principle. *You see, socialism is a failure, so now let's rid ourselves of all hints of it.* Individuation now rules. You're on your own. So now, in many organizations, we have the new work contract: We've got a relationship for as long as we've got a relationship. Develop your skills, because you can no longer count on the organization. If the integrating counterculture were to be completely suppressed as being out of touch with the demands of "new realities," systems will inevitably decay. Once the integrating glue is gone, loyalty will be to oneself and not to the system, and the predictable consequence of this will be that the system's best players will constantly be looking for greener fields for themselves.

System Leadership

System leaders—whether of the culture or the counterculture, whether in the political or the organizational worlds—have deep knowledge regarding the dynamics of system life. They see value in both the culture and the counterculture; they are not blind to the limitations of their system's primary orientation, and they understand the importance of incorporating the values of the other.

I said earlier (see "Politics and Preferences," Part III, Chapter 11) that I have a personal bias toward individuation. If I were in a system that condemned and suppressed individuation as "archaic, outmoded, patriarchal, that white-male thing," I would fight like the devil to have my orientation valued, and I would hope that I could do that while clearly valuing and, to the best of my ability, incorporating integration as needed by the system.

Changing environmental conditions may call for a shift toward greater individuation or greater integration; but the total suppression of either counterculture comes only at the peril of the system.

Lesson 1:

Discussion Questions and Activities

In your organization, are you part of the culture or the counterculture? Is your organizational function or your profession part of the culture or counterculture?

- Do you find yourself demonizing the other while glorifying the virtues of your own position?

- Do you find it easier to lead if you have an enemy, when you believe you are involved in righteous warfare?

- What do you have to give up or let go of in order to take a system leadership stand? If you are in a system committed to individuation, what do you have to give up or let go of in order to value and incorporate needed aspects of integration? Or if you are in a system committed to integration, what do you have to give up or let go of to value and make room for individuation?

- What emotional challenges does the system leadership role raise?

- Notice how system leaders—particularly in the political arena—run the risk of being seen as weak, as compromisers, as sellouts by the more zealous members of their culture or counterculture.

System Story III: The Terrible Dance of Power

Beyond the Power Lab

Several years ago a number of events came together that had a powerful impact on my thinking about systems and the implications for system leadership and membership.

At the time, there were daily news stories describing atrocities in hot spots throughout the world: Sri Lanka, Northern Ireland, El Salvador, Israel. Innocent victims were blown up in pubs and on buses, in cafes and in marketplaces; hung from lampposts, set afire, whole villages massacred. These were not wars against some external enemy (not that the existence of external enemies would justify such actions), this was internal warfare—citizen against citizen.

At the time I was least familiar with the turmoil in Sri Lanka, and was struck, like a deer caught in the headlights, reading the news coming from that country.

From the *Wall Street Journal*, November 3, 1988:

Sri Lanka's government imposed a nationwide night-time curfew in response to attacks by Sinhalese extremists that left at least 16 people dead. The Sinhalese militants, who oppose a government accord with minority Tamils, called a strike for today and vowed to kill those who defy it.

This was but the most recent event in a cycle of violence and counterviolence.

Tamil Tigers kill over 150 civilians in sacred Buddhist city....

The Tamil action has provoked the emergence of the JVP, an extremist Sinhalese organization, that is opposed to any concessions being made to the Tamil and killing those who do.

Similar bombings, murders, and assassinations were going on in Northern Ireland, Israel, El Salvador; and it was during this period that I was invited to give a presentation at a conference on organization development in international affairs. I immediately turned down the invitation. I was depressed by events in the world, feeling ignorant and powerless in the face of those events, and convinced that I had nothing to contribute. (Were not these feelings similar to those I had experienced prior to making my moves in New Hope? The difference here was that in regard to these international affairs, I was feeling depressed and powerless as a member in a much larger system— the world.) The host pressed me to reconsider, which I did reluctantly, and spent the next two months anxiously pondering what I would do.

Synchronicity Strikes

Three days before the program, still having no notion of what to do, I was rummaging through the shelves of the Boston Public Library looking for something to take my mind off my dilemma when I stumbled across a book that turned out to be my salvation. Here on the shelf was *War Zones*, a report by two journalists on five then-current war zones: Northern Ireland, El Salvador, Uganda, Israel, and Sri Lanka.[1] I stood at the stacks, devouring the book, experiencing one of those exhilarating-concepts moments.

News stories do not reveal the underlying System Story; they are more likely to mask it. Atrocities make the news; the configuration of events leading up to atrocities does not.

Reading the authors' accounts was like being an anthropologist at their side as they recalled the history of these conflicts and interviewed people on all sides. Here was another System Story emerging, another approximation of universal truths about ourselves and our systems, another set of archetypal themes and variations on these themes.

Over the weekend I put together my presentation for the conference. It was called "The Terrible Dance of Power" (a version of this is presented in *Seeing Systems*). In essence it told the story of systems in which there is a high power group and a low power group. The high power group has some noble mission for the system: manifest destiny, the master race, the true religion, the way. Standing in the way of this mission are the low power people. The struggle unfolds, beginning with the suppression of the low power people, followed by some mild protest from the low power people, followed by heightened oppression by the high power people, and gradually devolving into murderous and righteous warfare between radicals and moderates and extremists in both the high and low power groups. This is a story whose variations have played out in America with the gradual destruction of the American Indian; in Turkey with the destruction of the Armenians; in Germany with the destruction of the Jews, gypsies, and homosexuals; in China with the Cultural Revolution; in the Soviet Union with the extinction of millions of peasants; in Cambodia with the destruction of millions; in India with Hindus and Muslims massacring one another, and on and on. The story continues today. It is a most durable story.

What is My Place in the Larger Picture?

My personal experience was similar to my Power Lab experiences, only writ large. First there is the frustration, anxiety, and powerlessness, which I maintain is more than a personal experience; it is a systemic experience, a clue that there is something wrong with the system *and my relationship to it*. Then there is the clarity: I see this System Story and my relationship to it. It is clear that I am more than an observer of these systems; I am connected to them: to Sri Lanka, Israel, Northern Ireland,

Rwanda, and all the other places in which this System Story is playing out, and all the places where it might be played out in the future.

One of the consequences of exhilarating concepts is their power to take you to unexpected and sometimes painful places. I have been a longtime Zionist, proud of the incredible social, economic, and military accomplishments of the Israelis since 1948. Once I saw the dominant/other story as it was expressed in "The Terrible Dance," it was painfully clear to me that this was also a story being played out by my heroes. The power of System Stories is not in illuminating what you already know, but in revealing the previously unknown.

And finally there is the question of action. What can I do? This is not New Hope; there is no simple action I can take that will transform these systems; if there is, I have not yet seen it. I have great admiration for the peacemakers, those who are willing to wade right into the middle of seemingly intractable conflicts as they are raging, and who use all their mediation and negotiation skills in an effort to end the violence and carve out agreements aimed at enabling people to live in peace with one another. And maybe that is the best we can do.

I have another, parallel, mission. I envision a future in which there is no need to resolve these conflicts because they never arise in the first place, because people throughout the world see this System Story as they are living it, and they have the courage to step out of that story and create newer, saner, healthier, and more productive stories for themselves and their systems. My parallel path is education. My goal is to have the people of the world understand this System Story with all its destructive consequences, to have the story built into school curricula worldwide. To this end I have established The Terrible Dance of Power Web site, which posts "The Terrible Dance" and other items related to ethnic violence; I encourage people to distribute these items widely in areas of ethnic tension, translate them into other languages, send them to friends and colleagues in other countries, submit them to local newspapers, build dramatic presentations around them, organize ethnic-diversity dialogues in their neighborhoods and organizations, and more.[2]

I believe this is our next evolutionary challenge as human beings: to recognize ourselves as system creatures, to see the System Stories as we are living them, and to have the courage to step out of these stories and create newer, sane, healthy, and productive stories for ourselves and our systems. In the next chapter we explore the role of dominance in the Terrible Dance and in our efforts to create systems in which all members feel valued.

Lesson 2:

◊

And finally there is the question of what we all can do about the Terrible Dance. Once the System Story begins to unfold, it is difficult to stop. (Although peacemaking efforts are under way in such hot spots as Northern Ireland, Israel, South Africa, and Sri Lanka, the dance still continues, erupting in other hot spots such as Bosnia, Kosovo, Chechnya.) The cycle of recrimination and revenge, once begun, feeds on itself such that there is always justification for one more act of violence. This, then, demands Herculean and untiring efforts from the peacemakers. Their challenge is to have those engaged in the dance step out of the story and work together to create a new story.

The other challenge is to prevent the story from starting. This requires a revolutionary change in human consciousness: that all of us learn to see systems as wholes, recognize the destructive stories of the whole, and create new stories. System Stories are predictable; uncertainty develops when we step out of the predictable story and create a new story.

Try to envision a new story that begins, for example, when the Europeans first come to the Americas or when the Zionists first come to

Palestine, or in any of the other settings where the dance has happened or is happening. *First there is some great and noble vision, and others (lessers) are seen as standing in the way of that vision.* Envision what the world would look like if one were to step out of that story....

CHAPTER
16

System Story III
(continued):
The Dominants and the Others

Who wouldn't do this to such people?
From "The Terrible Dance of Power"

It is one thing to extol the virtues of a differenti-
ated system—its rich diversity of cultures, values,
lifestyles, ethnicity, spiritual practices, professional
specializations, entertainment and the arts, and
so forth. But diversity becomes problematic when
some differences are more equal than others.

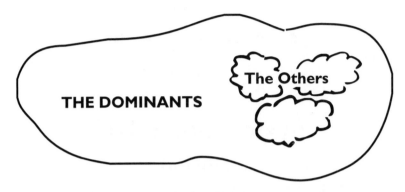

Trust Me; I Will Be Fair

I was meeting with a group of leaders from a government agency. I had presented them with the following statement and asked them to agree or disagree with it: "In matters of hiring, promotion and assignments, special consideration/protection should be given to women, minorities, and other traditionally overlooked groups."

Two-thirds of the group disagreed with the statement. Their position was that all people should be treated equally; that it is racist to give special consideration to people simply because they are members of some group; that it stigmatizes the very people you are trying to help (giving the impression that they are where they are *only* because of their group identity); that merit and competence are the only legitimate bases for hiring, promotion, and assignments; and that the mission of the system would be compromised if it were to be otherwise.

Those who agreed with the statement pointed out that the leadership group itself was all white (two-thirds male), and that that fact alone was testament to the need for special consideration/protection for traditionally overlooked groups. They maintained that in order to carry out its mission, the agency needed to come closer to mirroring the complexion of the general population, and that qualified minorities are likely to shy away from systems that have few people like them. And they argued that even the most fair-minded people unconsciously gave preference to people who look and speak and act like them.

It was this last point that most upset the others. *Trust me,* said one, *I* can *be fair and I* will *be fair.* Others expressed their agreement: good-hearted, well-intentioned people will be fair.

I have worked with these people; I know them to be decent, honorable, and well-intentioned. Still, the question remains: Can they be fair even when they intend to be fair? Which brings us to the matter of dominance.

The Invisible Differentiation

When we talk about diversity in systems, we usually refer to those who are often excluded—whether they are African Americans, Hispanics, gays and lesbians, women, the disabled, Native Americans, Asian Americans, immigrants, or others. It is as if the dominant culture is that which will incorporate the diversity of the Others, but it itself is not part of the diversity. To its members the dominant culture is the invisible differentiation. The Others are the differences, the diversity; the Dominants simply are what they are. The Dominants' culture, their culturally transmitted patterns—how they speak, how they interact, how they dress, their priorities, their pace of life, their standards of competence, their emotionality—all these are experienced by the Dominants not as options, not as quaint cultural quirks, but simply as the way things are. The Dominants have easier access to the system's valued resources by virtue of their being Dominants, and this relative ease of access is also invisible.

If the dominant culture is experienced not as an option but as the way things are, then how are Dominants likely to experience the different speech, pace, standards, patterns of interaction, emotionality, and dress of the Others? Will the Others be seen as quaint? interesting? something to emulate? Or will they be seen as not quite right? off? wrong speech, wrong dress, wrong emotionality, wrong values, wrong pace, wrong standards? And if that is the case, wouldn't it be possible for us to be unfair when we are sure we are being perfectly fair?

A Sampling of Dominant/Other Relationships

- People of color in a white-dominant system—society or organization
- Gays and lesbians in a heterosexual-dominant system
- Single mothers in a parent-couple-dominant system
- Albanians in a Serb-dominant system
- A low-status function (fill in the blank for your organization) in an organization in which a high-status function (fill in the blank) is dominant
- Arabs in a Jewish-dominant system
- Jews in a Christian-dominant system
- Disabled in an able-bodied system
- Hutus in a Tutsi-dominant system
- Russians in a Latvian-dominant system
- Native Americans in America
- French Canadians in an English Canadian-dominant system
- Chechnyans in a Russian-dominant system

So long as the Others remain out of the mainstream of the Dominant culture, they pose little problem to the Dominants; but as the Others become more prominent in the Dominant cultures—and insistent on their inclusion—tensions develop between the two groups.

Lesson 3:

Discussion

Many (most?) of us are neither pure Dominants nor pure Others; we are Dominant in some categories and Other in others. The chart below indicates several categories in which you could be either among the Dominants or an Other. Feel free to add other categories that are relevant to your situation.

	Gender	Race	Sexual Orientation	Physical Ability	Religion	Social Class	Organization Position	Region	Other
Dominant									
Other									

Indicate in each category whether you feel you are a Dominant or an Other. Have the members of your system complete the chart, and then meet in trios to discuss the following questions:

1. What are you discovering about your dominance and otherness?

2. How is your experience different when you are in the Dominant position as compared with when you are in the Other position?

3. When you are Dominant, how do you react to the Others' behavior? (Tell yourself the truth.) Do you have judgments and evaluations regarding the Others—their dress, speech, emotionality, attitude? What do they do that bothers you?

4.   In your reactions to the Others, do you see yourself as liberal (welcoming their difference) or conservative (wanting them to be more like the Dominants)? Or are you in some ways liberal and in others conservative? Describe.

5.   What is your experience when you are an Other in the Dominant world?

6.   What do the Dominants do that heightens your sense of Otherness? What settings heighten your sense of Otherness?

7.   How do you deal with your Otherness:

> do you become dysfunctional, tight, incompetent?

> do you try to adapt—to hide your Otherness, to look and act like the Dominants?

> do you withdraw?

> do you try to get back at or get even with the Dominants—castigating them or ignoring their traditions, rules, laws?

8.   In the story that introduced this section, one leader said, "Trust me, I can be fair; I will be fair." Have a conversation about that statement. Can the Dominants be fair? What are the barriers to fairness that even the most well-intentioned Dominant must face?

9.   What implications do the dynamics of dominance have for your role as system leader?

C H A P T E R
17

"I" and "US"

*There is a consciousness associated with Otherness,
what I call an "US" consciousness. The "US" consciousness is emotional; it has its own logic that is
not obvious to those who don't share that consciousness; it is historical such that past oppressions
live powerfully in the present; and it is global in
that when we are in the "US" consciousness, we
relate to one another not person to person but as
oppressed to oppressor.*

*The deeper one's history of oppression, the more
powerful is one's "US" consciousness and the more
readily it is brought to the surface.*

*If we are to create and maintain powerful
human systems, we need to understand and
respect one another's "US" consciousness.*

Differentiation + Dominance + the "US" Consciousness = Big Trouble

In this section I come full cycle. This book has been about
lessons from the Power Lab—my lessons and yours. But now it is
time for us to take a closer look at who is this teacher of lessons. I

can understand how you might have two views of me: from my Power Lab stories, you might see me as a playful imp making trouble (and stirring up interest) for himself and others; from my theoretical work you might see me as a cold scientist standing outside of systems and developing passionless frameworks for making sense of system life. Both may be true, yet both miss what drives my work. I am an educator, yet what drives me in education is not what I know, but what I desperately need to know in order to at least make sense of this world, if not to change it. I have a passion to understand a world that has bewildered me and that continues to bewilder me. Some stories:

I was a lad of fourteen working in my father's store in Boston's West End (no longer existent); it was just months after the end of World War II. A disgruntled customer standing by the front door was arguing with my uncle, who was standing toward the rear of the store, with me between the two, quite close to the customer. The customer had the final word when he shouted at my uncle, "The trouble with Hitler is that he didn't kill *all* the Jews," and then stormed out. Did he really mean that? Did he really wish that my uncle and I and all the rest of Jews were dead? Could this man standing so close to me have joined happily as an accomplice in the Holocaust? What allowed him, or drove him, to say that? I have needed to understand that.

Even at a younger age, there was a gang from a nearby area who periodically would chase after us Jews, calling us "Christ killers." It was clear to me that *I* didn't kill anyone (at that time I had little understanding of who Christ was); and I suspected that these gang members knew *I* hadn't killed anyone, yet something was driving them. I needed to understand that.

Jumping ahead many years, Karen Oshry, Anne Litwin, Bill Woodson, and I were developing our newest program, Creating Community in the Face of Difference. My goal was to make some contribution to system sanity in an era in which "difference" was exacting terrible tolls—ethnic cleansing in Bosnia, holocausts in Rwanda and Burundi, continuing warfare in Israel and Northern Ireland, calls for separatism among the Kurds, Basques, and French Canadians, and our continuing struggles in America around differences in race, class, and sexual orientation.

This was to be a program in which my passions lay, yet there came a point when I felt I should withdraw from that program. I felt too biased, too locked into a white perspective; I felt that I was incapable of needed objectivity, that I was ignorant beyond the possibility of learning.

What triggered these feelings was the jury's decision on the O.J. Simpson murder trial. Simpson had been an all-American football player; he went on to become a leading running back in the National Football League; upon retirement he acted in several movies and became television spokesman for a major automobile rental agency. Simpson, an African American, had been accused of murdering his ex-wife, Nicole Brown Simpson, and Ron Goldman, both white. The jury's verdict had the effect of a perfect system power move in that it demonstrated with a jeweler's precision just how wide the gap was between white and black America. There were televised scenes of jubilant blacks and depressed whites at the moment the verdict was delivered. To many (not all) whites, the evidence against Simpson, plus his history of wife battering, was overwhelming; it was inconceivable to them that a largely (not totally) black jury could have ignored all that evidence. To many (not all) blacks, this was so clearly a case of Simpson's being framed by a racist detective.

I could deal with arguments about the validity of the evidence, but there was one response I couldn't handle. My hackles went up whenever a black said, "It's about time." *What do you mean, "It's about time"? What has that got to do with anything? Either he did it or he didn't. This is not about rectifying past injustices; this is about here and now. He did it or he didn't; that's all that should matter.*

It was at that point that I felt I should withdraw from the staff of the Creating Community program. How could I provide leadership when I was so firmly entrenched in my camp and the Other was completely incomprehensible to me? Then two events occurred.

I am sitting in an airplane reading. I am in my "I" consciousness—living in the present, going about my business, making my solitary way in the world. I overhear a conversation several rows behind me—two men speaking German. I become agitated, annoyed. It's that language. I am angry at these two men whom I can't even see. They are part of something else, something that extends beyond them and beyond the present and beyond the space of this airplane—a history of anti-Semitism ("You killed Christ"), collaboration in the Holocaust, the murder of innocents. My anger is not just at them…it is at their kind.

My consciousness has shifted uncontrollably; I can no longer concentrate on my book; I am no longer "I", I am now "US"— Jews. A very different consciousness. The "US" is broad and deep. I feel connected to it all—the old men in the synagogues, the prayers, the mysteries, the death camps, the Israeli wars, the songs and festivals.

The "US" is drenched in emotionality. Anger. Righteousness. Where was my logic? Who were these two men that I should feel anger toward them? What had *they* done? For all I knew, they themselves were Jews (there are still Jews in Germany) or sympathizers or possibly even active protesters against anti-Semitism. The "US" consciousness is historic; it extends far beyond the limits of my lifetime; the past exists powerfully in the present; the triumphs and sins of the past continue to live in the here and now.

The "US" consciousness is rich, emotional, historic, global (we are no longer dealing person to person; we are now category to category—black to white, Jew to gentile, gay to heterosexual, and so forth). All Others have their powerful "US" consciousness. We are easily clicked into it.

I am having a pleasant dinner with a colleague. We have known one another for years; several times she has been instrumental in bringing our work into her organization. The conversation turns to the richness of biological diversity. "What do you think accounts for it?" she asks. "Evolution," I say. She disagrees. "What, then?" I ask. "Creationism," she says. She then goes on to witness for me the power of prayer, the miracle when all doctors said it was hopeless. God intervened and saved the child. Zap! She said the magic word, "prayer," and now I'm back into it. Prayer. The power of prayer. How can you say such a thing? Why didn't your god answer the prayers of 6 million Jews, and why was your god so quiet the night before the gypsies were murdered and it was said that their cries rose up to heaven? Was he deaf on that night? *"What could he have done?" she said. "A miracle," I said, "just like you say he did for your friend." And so ended a pleasant evening, a missed opportunity to learn more about her and her faith, a missed opportunity for me to share my own beliefs, a missed opportunity to deepen our relationship by hearing and respecting our differences. Instead the evening ended in uncomfortable silence.*

Just say the magic word—kike, nigger, mick, spic, jap, fag, dyke; bring up ancient or current oppression—lynching, holocaust, concentration camp, stereotype, persecution, exclusionary laws, cemetery desecration; mention the historic enemy—whitey, Serb, Muslim, Hutu, Tutsi, Jew, gay basher, fascist: and there we are again, out of the "I" and into the "US." The "I" is no match for the "US"; it is easily swept away. Dangerous demagogues (political leaders, not system leaders) of past and present gain their strength by doing this to us all the time.

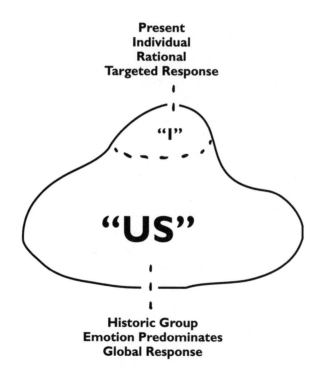

**Present
Individual
Rational
Targeted Response**

"I"

"US"

**Historic Group
Emotion Predominates
Global Response**

The "US" consciousness lies at the heart of the Dominant/Other relationship, and no real transformation of that relationship is possible without recognizing and dealing with that consciousness. Actions that flow out of the "US" consciousness of the Others are irrational to the "I" consciousness of the Dominants.

Why do rioting prisoners make their cells unlivable?

Why would ghetto residents destroy their own neighborhoods?

Why does Barry get so angry when a friend talks about her faith?

Why do terrorists murder innocents?

Why do oppressed turn against their supporters?

To the Dominants all these actions are experienced as irrational and are further evidence of the inferiority of the Other. Yet all these actions have their logic within the "US" consciousness.

The "US" consciousness is universal. The Buddha said that life is tough, and so it is, and since time immemorial we have been desperately seeking the oppressor who has made it so. Most, if not all, of us know the Other experience—some with a small "o" and some with a giant one. Most, if not all, of us are victims of one sort or another—victims of the government, the gentiles, the colonialists, the white man, the Jew, the Protestants, the Turks, the West, the Serbs; and wherever there is a history of victimization, there is the "US" consciousness ready to be tapped. I use the term "victimization" not in the negative sense of nonresponsibility for our lives; on the contrary, I mean *real* victimization. People have done terrible things to our various "US"es: they have enslaved us, deprived us of our rights, sent us off to fight evil wars, humiliated us, stolen our property, taxed us unfairly, driven us from our homes, separated us from our families, imprisoned us, excluded us, tortured and murdered us. All of this is real, and all of this is stored in our "US" consciousness. Nor am I implying that since we are all victims, all victimizations are equal—the oppression of being heavily taxed or made to register my handgun is real, yet it in no way measures up to that of being forced from our homes, lynched, or gassed.

We can all tap into our "US" consciousness, but for some of us that consciousness is more part and parcel of our everyday experience—being a person of color in a white-dominant society; a woman in a male-dominant organization; gay, lesbian, or bisexual in a heterosexual-dominant culture; Palestinian in an Israeli-dominant culture; Albanian in a Serb-dominant culture, and so forth.

It is the "US" consciousness of the Other that we must understand and be prepared to deal with if we are to lead and be members of systems in which all of us feel full membership. When we suppress the Other's "US" consciousness, when we do not allow it to be heard and respected, when we insist on the predominance of our own "US" consciousness (my victimization is greater than yours), then communication breaks down. It is the suppression of the "US" consciousness that outrages the Other; and where there is no communication or understanding, anger and violence are sure to follow.

Lesson 4:

◊

The purpose of the following exercises is to help you and other system members learn about one another's "US" consciousness. There are two lessons. The first is a set of exercises for use with a system in which you are leader or member. This must be a system in which there is some diversity—gender, ethnicity, sexual orientation, religion, physical ability—and in which members are willing to work on their feelings and attitudes toward diversity. The second set of exercises asks you to explore the implications of "US" consciousness for ethnic, racial, and religious trouble spots around the world.

I.   *Working with your system.* (This exercise is based on the work of my colleague Anne Litwin, and is presented here with her permission.)

Step 1: Have each member identify his/her Otherness. Encourage members to choose the Otherness identity that has the most energy for them, that is, the one for which the "US" consciousness is most sensitive—religion, ethnicity, gender, age, physical ability, sexual orientation. *Caution members to choose an identity they are willing to talk about publicly.*

Have members form common-identity groups. Some members may feel that they have no Otherness in their lives. If so, have them listen to the conversation that follows. Listening to others may remind them of arenas in which they do feel their Otherness. Have those who do not identify any area of Otherness form themselves into a "Pure Dominants" group.

Even if there is only one person in a group, encourage that person to handle the following activities alone.

Step 2: Give each group thirty minutes to answer the questions below. Have one person in each group be the recorder. Stress the importance of capturing the group's work because each group will be reporting to the whole. Encourage members to tell the truth about their Otherness (and Pure Dominant) experiences.

A. In what ways are the members of your group similar? (When thinking about "your group," consider both the people who are here with you now as well as the larger group.)

B. In what ways are the members of your group different? (Again, think in terms of those who are here and those who are not.)

C. What events in your group's past are still with you in the present? Past tragedies? Past triumphs?

D. How often and under what conditions do you feel your "US" consciousness?

E. What is important to you about this identity? What don't you want to lose?

F. What is offensive to members of your group? What actions, words, events, attitudes, and beliefs upset them?

Step 3: Each group has approximately ten minutes to report its work. The instructions for other groups at this time are:

Just listen and try to understand.

It is permissible for listeners to ask questions for clarification, but what is not permissible are debates, arguments, evaluations, or justifications.

In your conversations, do your best to avoid competition for victim status, that is, "I'm more oppressed than you are."

Step 4: Give yourselves twenty to thirty minutes to discuss what you heard.

1. What similarities and differences do you see among the groups?

2. What was your experience in being able to talk about your "US" consciousness?

3. What are your reactions to what you heard? What are you learning?

II. *Implications for system leadership.* As our systems become increasingly diverse, there is an increased risk of members' triggering one another's "US" consciousness, often unknowingly. Consider the hypothesis: We need to understand one another's "US" consciousness, but to resolve problems we need to react "I" to "I."

1. Do you think that "US" sensitivities currently exist in a system in which you are leader or member (for example, around issues of gender, sexual orientation, race, physical ability, religion)? How do you deal with these? Do you avoid discussing them? Just be pleasant to

everyone? If your goal is to live in a system in which all members feel part of the whole with their differences respected and valued, what is your strategy for addressing issues of "US" consciousness? How does your strategy map with the above hypothesis?

2. Let's say that through the United Nations you are given the leadership assignment of developing a long-term strategy for resolving one of the more intractable issues of our time: conflicts between Israelis and Palestinians, Northern Ireland Catholics and Protestants, Greek and Turkish Cypriots, Hindus and Muslims in India, or any of the ethnic conflicts in the Balkans. All sides in these conflicts have long and deep experiences of oppression. What would be the key elements in your strategy?

3. If one of your leadership roles is as a parent, how do you prepare your child(ren) for the "US" consciousness they will encounter in the world?

Epilogue:

An Experiment That Did Not Fail

System power is the ability to act

as if you can make happen

whatever it is you want to have happen,

knowing that you cannot,

and being willing to live with and work with

whatever does happen.

INTRODUCTION

After all we have gone through in the previous sections, I feel you deserve a culminating event, something that brings it all together in a perfect demonstration of the power of all this work. Instead, I will leave you with a less than perfect tale of system power and leadership: an action that did not succeed...nor did it completely fail.

I tell the story because it is a leadership move. And it may have particular significance because it comes from a Bottom position. You will recognize many of the elements of power moves that are described in previous sections: the feelings of a system member (me)—anxiety, fear, depression, anger; the use of these feelings as clues to the condition of the system and my relationship to it; and an effort to change my relationship to the system and the system itself. The aim of this move was to bring an entire system to awareness and produce fundamental system change. It came up short in many respects, yet it did produce remarkable results. For these reasons I call it an experiment that did not fail.

This is an insider's story of the power move; there is no anthropologist to give us a detached total system picture. In making the power move, I did my best to be both insider (using my experiences in the system) and outsider (providing a more detached and analytic picture of the system), but there are obvious limitations to my objectivity. Given that, here is my tale.

Down and Out in Organizational Life

This is a story of how I was abused, humiliated, and fired from my job, and how I responded to all of that.

Some years ago I was working for an organization; I believed I was making significant contributions—developing new programs and theoretical frameworks—but the Tops were dissatisfied with my performance; I was not bringing in enough money. I felt I was an important research and development operation that was being evaluated by production standards, and that my fate was being decided not by professional associates who might understand and value my work but by administrators and accountants who were simply looking at the immediate bottom line. In the middle of salary negotiations my paychecks were cut off without notice—the checks simply stopped coming—which I felt was uncommonly cruel, particularly in light of the humanistic values espoused by this organization. I felt powerless, angry, and afraid. Shortly thereafter the check-stopping was formalized; I was fired. Months of depression followed. I lost my confidence. I felt I no longer had anything to contribute. My work suffered. After many painful months, I got back on my feet, and Karen and I founded Power & Systems, Inc.

A few years later the president of the organization that fired me and I established a new business relationship that we believed offered benefits to both organizations, but before that arrangement could be put into place, there was a "palace coup" —the president was tossed out, new leadership positions were put into place, and our business relationship was overturned. There was no conversation, no explanation; the arrangement simply did not fit with the "new directions." More anger, more depression.

I steered clear of the organization for several years, all the while harboring deep resentment over how I felt I had been treated. Then I was invited to enter into still another form of partnership with that same organization. (Here the reader must wonder, with good reason, why with such a history I would even consider any arrangement; the attraction, however, was powerful. There was always the possibility that association with this prestigious organization could enhance the prospects of my own fledgling organization.) I accepted, and once again the relationship ended in disaster.

Two infuriating pieces of news arrived in the same letter from headquarters. The first was a two-sentence dismissal of a proposal that I felt was critical to our future and that Karen and I had worked very hard to develop. (The proposal was to institute the business relationship that the previous president had accepted.) The answer from headquarters was a flat No, and the rationale was essentially "...our policy has been...and therefore our policy will be..." And that was the end of it. The second piece of news concerned a programmatic decision that headquarters had earlier committed to supporting. Now we found that headquarters, without any discussion with us, reversed their earlier position and ruled against us.

For two days we tried to reach people at headquarters. Our phone calls were not returned—we were told that people were tied up in important meetings and they would get back to us, but they didn't. Only after repeated badgering ("Tell Richard [a fictitious name] that I hope he would have the common courtesy to return my fourth phone call") did we finally get through. When I reached one party, he assured me that the final decision (the reversal) had not yet been made and that he was not involved in the decision. When we reached the second party, we were assured that the final decision *had* been made and that the first party had been fully involved in it. Someone had lied.

That evening I seethed in anger and frustration: we had been dismissed, flicked away like pesky flies; the concept of "partnership" had been a sham; our positions, our thoughts, our feelings, our wishes, none of these mattered. There appeared to be no rationale to headquarters' decisions. Simply No. Yet all this was done with great friendliness—"I hope we can continue our current relationship....Love to you and Karen...."

I was outraged—"You can take your love and..." This two-paragraph letter was merely the triggering event; it brought back all the anger and frustration and humiliation I had experienced over the past several years—the lack of respect for my work, having decisions about its value being made by an accountant, having my paycheck cut off in the middle of salary negotiations, being fired, lied to, dealt with in what seemed to me to be a mindless bureaucratic fashion.

The Move Begins to Take Shape

That night I slept fitfully. You will by now recognize the process.

At 4 A.M. an idea came to me, and throughout the early morning it continued to take shape. A plan was emerging, an outrageous plan. It was to be my revenge, but it was to be much more than that. I was excited, mobilized ... and afraid. Could I pull this off? And if I did, how would others react? Would they see me as crazy? Would they dismiss me as a self-righteous whiner? A poor loser?

A Systems Letter

The idea was to write a letter; but this was to be a new kind of letter, an invention in communication, a systems letter. The letter would put the current situation in its systemic context. I would send this letter to over 300 people—the current membership of the organization, colleagues who had dropped out in dissatisfaction, the current leadership, past leadership, and other interested parties. I was struck with the possibilities of such a communication: it would enable me to air my particular grievance, and it could move much beyond that. I could use my experience as a Bottom to shed light on the bottom experiences of others, to illuminate the life of this particular system, and to illuminate system life generally.

Leader as Insider and Outsider

I would write this letter as an insider, describing my feelings of outrage and betrayal, using these feelings not as evidence of my personal problems but as cues to the condition of the system and as leverage for changing the system and my relationship to it. And I would write it as an outsider, standing aside of the system, detached from it, describing the whole, its current form, its history, and how the current situation connected with that history. The letter would be deeply personal—my "cry from the heart"—one member's unvarnished tale of woe. And it would be solidly analytical, a clear and dispassionate view of the system's history, structure, and processes. The possibilities of the letter overwhelmed me. I could make this system visible to all of us—past and present members—and I could do it in a way that would shed light not only on my condition but on the experiences of all of us.

Doubts Creep In

Could I do this? As I lay in bed or paced the floor in these early morning hours, thoughts flooded in on me: I saw the system, I saw the historical processes that had brought us to this point, I saw the systemic factors that were shaping my consciousness and that of others in the system. But I was afraid. I was afraid that I couldn't contain all of this complexity, that I wouldn't be able to shape it into a coherent and engaging story, and that even if I did, no one would care.

Synchronicity Strikes

I went to the post office that morning still uncertain as to whether to proceed. Should I undertake this letter or just swallow my anger—as we so often do in our bottomness—and move on? Will others see me as crazy? *Am I crazy?* As the fates would have it, in my mailbox that morning was a brochure announcing a workshop on women and stress, and the title of one presentation caught my eye: "A Healthy Woman Is A Crazy Person!" That settled it for me. A Healthy System Member Is Also A Crazy Person!

The System Letter Unfolds

For the next three days the systems letter poured out of me; I had never before written so clearly or powerfully with so few pauses to think or edit. It was as if the letter—or the system—were writing itself. In the letter I attempted to put all of our experiences in a systemic context. The following are some examples.

The Revolt of the Counterculture

One particular aspect of the system's history struck me with great clarity. We had been living a variation of the culture/counterculture System Story. For years the culture of the organization had been this: the president made unilateral decisions regarding assignment and opportunities; he regularly chose those people whom he regarded as most competent and whom he trusted. As a consequence, the system consisted of two groups: members who were given assignments with great regularity (I felt privileged to be in that group) and those who were called on rarely if at all. There were constant complaints from the underused; they were in essence the integrating counterculture of the system, pressing for equality of opportunity, democratizing the system, pressing for involvement in decision making. But the demands of this group went largely unrecognized—until the president retired. Then came the revolt of the counterculture, the palace coup.

I was on the losing end of this battle. I had been living in the world where the president could decide, but that world was gone. There would be no more unilateral decision making; decisions were to be made by networks of committees. My new arrangement was too special, too unique for this egalitarian order. Individuation was out. I described my condition and that of the other previously privileged members as follows:

> We were czarists whose mansions and estates were about to be converted into lodging houses, schools and day care centers. Ugh! How tasteless, how totally devoid of class (in both senses of the word)....Not for us that world of socialist sacrifice for the state, of decisions by committee, of constraint by our peers, of living by the rules; so we raised our noses, packed up our kits, and huffed away....
>
> [The organization is] broader in spectrum as a membership body than we have ever been, and we are more politically involved in our destinies than we have ever been. Yet, as we know from all socialist revolutions, there

are costs to this change as well as gains. Some of us are oblivious to those costs because they are not *our* costs; this system is fine for us. It is our structure, it fits our energies well…. Yet, for others of us, this is not our structure; it limits us, it constrains us, we are not free to move around; we feel suffocated by mutual control; we feel homogenized. And like all dissenters to socialism, like Sakharov, Solzhenitzyn, Ginsburg, et al., we are seen as dangerous, we are misunderstood, we are viewed as lunatics, and, in the end, we are constrained, confined, destroyed, or banished.

Topness and Bottomness

I wanted both to express my anger at the system's president and to put that anger in an analytic context. Addressing myself to the president, I wrote:

> For us Bottoms, life is relatively simple, uncomplex. We focus on the relatively narrow band of responsibility which is ours, and we do what we are supposed to do; we manufacture or we service or we create. We have our problems here, but if there is one virtue to our lives, it is their simplicity.
>
> Whereas the life of a Top is quite different; there are inputs coming at us from all directions and in different shapes and forms. Our lives are a sea of complexity….We must simplify our world or we will be overwhelmed by it. And in simplifying our world we look for numbers, for criteria, for simple bases for establishing priorities, for making evaluations and decisions….But, inevitably, unless we are incredibly wise or unless we have developed remarkable means for staying in close touch with our Bottoms, our systems of organization, our mechanisms for ordering complexity, are going to be out of touch with the realities as experienced by our Bottoms. To them, our bases of priority-setting, evaluation, and action often seem off the mark; we seem to have

squeezed the juice out of their work. They are bewildered, they feel misunderstood, they are outraged.... And we are stunned by their reactions....Given the complex demands of our life, we have performed a Herculean task. We are hurt by their rage; we are stung; we feel misunderstood....

So what's a Bottom to do? Forgive and forget? Understand and empathize with the world of our Tops even when their actions do us serious injustice? What commodity is more highly prized than loyalty and obedience? But, you see, there is a greater and more highly valued gift I can offer you, and that all of us can offer our Tops. We can give you our rage. We can become visible to you; we can tell you how aloof, distant, mechanistic, arrogant, and arbitrary you are; and we can tell you how much you have demeaned us and ripped away our self-respect. We can tell you this not because we hate you, although in the moment that may be true; we can tell you this not because we want to hurt you, although in the moment that may also be true; we can tell you this not because we want to tear down your system, although in the moment that may also be true. But we can tell you this for no other reason than to offer you the gift of clarity, so that you see what you have never seen before, and know what you have never known before.

The Power of Clarity

The final letter was 87 pages long. When I was done, it was done. All the anger, frustration, powerlessness—they were gone. Toward the end of the letter I wrote:

I was outraged. Well, that is done now. Gone. It is important to understand what happened to that rage. I have not psychoanalyzed it away, pounded pillows, primal screamed, or meditated it away, although each of these might have helped. Nor have I met and confronted each and every one of you to work through the intricacies of our individual sets of interpersonal relationships, although doing that might also have helped. My rage disappeared through an entirely different process; it disappeared through clarifying the nature of my systemic existence. By becoming clearer about the system—IT—and about ITs particular configuration of processes and structures, I also became clearer about me and my interpersonal relations with others. And this is the essence of my systemic orientation.

The Aftermath

I call the system letter "an experiment that did not fail." It did not succeed if success was measured by a fundamental transformation of the system, which would have made room in this integrating culture for the individuating energy I and others brought, if there were fundamental changes in the ways Tops and Bottoms related in the system. There was a flurry of activity within the organization: some angry letters and calls flowed into headquarters, there were some heated exchanges among board members; there was talk of reorganization, committees to be established, and so forth. I know very little of what, if anything, came of it all, since one consequence of the system letter was that I was done with the organization. The emotional connection—both my love and rage—were gone. I had no further interest in it and no desire to connect with it in any way.

I heard from friends that some readers were puzzled by the letter, some didn't understand it, and others thought I was crazy (literally). Over the next few months I was flooded with letters and phone calls (some phone calls coming in the middle of the night from excited readers who had just finished the letter and couldn't wait until morning to call). There were some mild rebukes. One criticism was that I wasn't sufficiently understanding or appreciative of Tops; another was that since I wrote the story, it was too easy for me to write myself in as hero. (Undoubtedly true.) And there was some well-meaning advice about what else I should do with my life and how I ought not to have allowed myself to be so hurt by any organization. Most responses were positive, some were downright effusive: "a virtuoso experiment in change," "a noble experiment in system consciousness raising"; others expressed admiration for my "integrity," "honesty," "conceptualizing," and—I think it's praise—"vulnerability." People thanked me for helping them see that system and all systems more clearly.

People also sent me their poetry and other writings and gifts along with outpourings of feeling. The most common theme in the letters had to do with people's experiences as outraged members both in this and in other organizations—feeling unappreciated, humiliated, and abused by unseeing, uncaring, and unresponsive systems.

It was surprising to me, although I suppose it shouldn't have been, to find that so many of the responses came from the "stars" in the field, people we don't normally think of as oppressed organization members. The founder of the organization wrote to me of his anguish.

> At my retirement deliberate crude efforts were made to dehumanize, humiliate, and deprive me. Former employees whom I had known for years were forbidden to have any communication with me. Naturally, this created the rage and anger you express so well, particularly at the crudeness, deliberateness, and dehumanization of the effort.

Another past president of the organization wrote:

> It pained and cleansed me to read your letter since I have been through much of the same complexities of feelings. I chose to work through my anguish in therapy. I've never figured out [this organization's] sickness, of which I was a part and for which I have many regrets.

Another one of the founders wrote of his resigning from the organization:

> ...because IT, which had been so important to me, *and important because of me,* had become a very hurtful relationship.

I heard from members who had quit the organization and others who had been fired, as well as from current members and staff. An administrative assistant wrote:

> It helped me to remember that I'm not crazy either even though [the organization] has at times made me think I was.

Several people resonated with my experience of being mindlessly blocked by "Our policy has been…therefore our policy will be…" Letters came in from strangers: "[So and so] gave me your letter. Thanks. I knew it was meant for me." And then would follow their story of oppression. Another unintended recipient to whom the letter was passed by an organization member described my action as poking my lance at the windmill.

> The windmill probably won't fall or even quiver, but you took an honest shot and probably will never know *all* the good you did.

I hoped that was the case. From the 360 letters sent, I received written responses from 87 people and phone calls from about two dozen more.

The letter was written more than twenty years ago, yet today I still run across people who reread the letter periodically as a way of grounding themselves in their own system lives.

The system letter may not have been the system-change success I had hoped it would be; but as a move it wasn't bad.

Lessons from the Power Lab

So what are my lessons from the Power Lab?

- *System leadership is a possibility from whatever system position you are in.* Position is not the determining factor; the determining factors are: *belief* that you can make a difference, a deep *understanding* of systems, and the *courage* to act.

- *Lead from the inside.* You are not a visitor to your systems, you are *of* these systems, they run through you. Let your systems wash over you. Attend to your feelings. Use these feelings as clues to the condition of your systems and your relationship to them, and as cues to what action you need to take.

- *Seek to bring the system to an awareness of itself.* The system power move reveals the system to its members—the "elephants in the room," the critical issues that are not being faced—and thus creates the possibility of enlightened system action by members.

- *Seek freedom within the context of system life.* Seize the opportunity of the moment. Beware of the tugs of your role, your history, the expectations of others, or the pull of systemic conditions, all of which may constrain you from action, or even blind you to the possibilities before you. Risk looking a bit strange if that is what it takes to make happen what the system needs to have happen.

In another stroke of synchronicity, on the morning I was writing this final section, I came across the obituary of William H. Whyte, author of *The Organization Man* (1956). Whyte wrote, "We are describing [the organization's] defects as virtues and denying that there is—or should be—a conflict between the individual and the organization. The denial is bad for the organization and worse for the individual.... Fight the organization, but not self-destructively. I write with the optimistic premise that individualism is possible in our times as in others. I speak of individualism within organizational life."

- *Lead from the outside.* Be the detached observer of your system. See the whole of it, know its history—how it got to this point—understand the culture and the counterculture and where you are in all of that. Notice what processes of the whole are missing or are being undervalued, and be a force for bringing these into the system.

- *Do not politicize system processes.* And beware of those who do. When it comes to individuation and integration, differentiation and homogenization, stabilization and change, there are no good or bad, better or worse, processes. They are all valuable contributions to system health. Politicization tends to devalue and dismiss certain individuals and their potential contributions.

- *Add energy to your list of values.* Consider the value of system moves that bring you and others to life, that sharpen system issues that are not being dealt with, that can unfreeze the system. Energizing moves may at times come up against other values you hold, such as consensus, participation, trust. Be aware when those competing values deaden you and others, limit the growth opportunities for you and them, and maintain the system status quo.

- *Be aware of the System Stories (Top/Middle/Bottom, Culture/ Counterculture, Terrible Dance) as you are living them.* Notice how the System Stories limit your possibilities in the system and the possibilities of the system. Power comes from stepping out of the predictable System Story and creating an unpredictable new story.

- *Be aware of the culture and counterculture in your system.* Whether you are in the culture or counterculture, beware of glorifying your own position, demonizing that of the other, and dismissing the value that the other offers your system.

- *Notice the roles that dominance and otherness play in system life.* Notice your experiences when you are Dominant and when you are Other. Be sensitive to your own and others'

"US" consciousness. Honor the "US" consciousness, but resolve your issues "I" to "I."

- *Do not expect systems to work like clockworks;* they are more like energy fields. Your moves are not likely to bring about the precise results you were intending. But *something* always happens—look for that something and work with it.

With the belief that we can change our systems, a deep understanding of system process, and the courage to act, systems cannot help but change.

There was a point at the end of the system letter where I wrote

God, I suddenly stopped. There was an incredible stillness in me and around me. I know that I am finished. It is 7:20 P.M., Friday, May 4, 1979, and my systems letter is finished.

So now I say: There is an incredible stillness in me and around me. It is 7:44 P.M., Tuesday, January 12, 1999, and my lessons from the Power Lab are finished.

N O T E S

Prologue:

1. Barry Oshry, *Power and Position* (Boston: Power & Systems, 1977).

2. Barry Oshry, *The Possibilities of Organization* (Boston: Power & Systems, 1986).

3. Barry Oshry, *Space Work* (Boston: Power & Systems, 1992).

4. Barry Oshry, *In the Middle* (Boston: Power & Systems, 1994).

5. Barry Oshry, *Seeing Systems: Unlocking the Mysteries of Organizational Life* (San Francisco: Berrett-Koehler, 1995).

Introduction:

1. Our partners in this program were members of the Race Institute of Baltimore, Maryland; this was a dedicated group of men and women, black and white, whose focus was on racism in institutional life. It was the Race Institute's experience with lunches (some guests were given elaborate meals and others had meager offerings or nothing at all) that led us to experiment with the Have/Have Not society design, in which we would extend this notion to encompass all aspects of participants' lives.

2. In 1972 the Power Lab moved to the Craigville Conference Center on Cape Cod in Massachusetts and has remained there ever since. Craigville, a self-contained village with a variety of houses and meeting spaces and a very supportive staff, has been an ideal setting for creating a societal experience.

PART I: Chapter 1

1. Since this first program was intended to focus on a variety of forms of institutional oppression—racism, sexism, ageism—we assembled a diverse training staff. Three years before our program, Betty Friedan had written *The Feminine Mystique*, (New York: Norton, 1963), which brought feminism and issues of gender discrimination and oppression back onto the American stage (and eventually the world stage) with great power. Betty was a founder and first president of the National Organization for Women. A bonus for us was that as a student of Virginia Satir, Betty was knowledgeable about experiential-learning technology; her male beauty contest was just one of her many design contributions.

2. James Kunen had just graduated from Columbia University where he had been an astute observer of the 1968 student uprising, which he chronicled in *The Strawberry Statement: Notes of a College Revolutionary*, (New York: Random House, 1969) a trenchant view of the youth culture of the times.

3. For more on loose and tight, and interaction comfort, see my *Power and Position*, pp. 31–42.

Chapter 2

1. See Tom Wicker's description of the Attica prison uprising—in which, for many prisoners, a doomed rebellion was preferable to the hopeless, numbing routine of prison life—in *A Time to Die* (New York: Quadrangle/New York Times, 1975).

2. See Ryan Malan, *My Traitor's Heart* (London: Bodley Head, 1990). South Africa at the time struck me as a high-stakes, all-encompassing Power Lab.

Chapter 4

1. Barry Oshry, *In the Middle*

2. Paulo Freire, *Pedagogy of the Oppressed* (London: Penguin Books, 1972).

PART III: Chapter 12

1. I have omitted change and stabilization from this analysis, since there is no systemic condition driving any one of these three systems to be more or less imbalanced than any other on the change/stabilization dimension.

PART IV: Chapter 15

1. Jon Lee Anderson and Scott Anderson, *War Zones* (New York: Dodd, Mead & Company, 1988).

2. See the Terrible Dance Web site: www.terribledanceofpower.org.

I N D E X

About the Author

Barry Oshry is president of Power & Systems, Inc., a Boston-based educational institution he and his wife and partner, Karen Ellis Oshry, established in 1975.

A pioneer in systems thinking, he has developed high-impact programs aimed at illuminating system life and empowering system members at all levels and in all positions. He is the creator of The Power Lab (The Power & Leadership Conference), which is offered twice yearly on Cape Cod in Massachusetts; The Organization Workshop on Creating Partnership, which he and Power & Systems associates conduct in organizations and institutions throughout the world; and the workshop on Creating Community in the Face of Difference. His other activities include the Rabination Project and the Terrible Dance of Power Web site. His essay "The Terrible Dance of Power" and his book *The Dance of Disempowerment* have been the bases of productions by the Seattle Public Theater and the Seattle Mime Company. His most recent venture is writing and staging the play *Organization Life*.

Barry Oshry can be reached at:
Power & Systems, Inc.
P.O. Box 990288
Prudential Station
Boston, Massachusetts 02199-0288
Phone: 617-437-1640
Fax: 617-437-6713
E-mail: boshry18@aol.com or info@powerandsystems.com
Web address: www.powerandsystems.com

Berrett-Koehler Publishers

BERRETT-KOEHLER is an independent publisher of books, periodicals, and other publications at the leading edge of new thinking and innovative practice on work, business, management, leadership, stewardship, career development, human resources, entrepreneurship, and global sustainability.

Since the company's founding in 1992, we have been committed to supporting the movement toward a more enlightened world of work by publishing books, periodicals, and other publications that help us to integrate our values with our work and work lives, and to create more humane and effective organizations.

We have chosen to focus on the areas of work, business, and organizations, because these are central elements in many people's lives today. Furthermore, the work world is going through tumultuous changes, from the decline of job security to the rise of new structures for organizing people and work. We believe that change is needed at all levels—individual, organizational, community, and global—and our publications address each of these levels.

We seek to create new lenses for understanding organizations, to legitimize topics that people care deeply about but that current business orthodoxy censors or considers secondary to bottom-line concerns, and to uncover new meaning, means, and ends for our work and work lives.

See next page for other books from Berrett-Koehler Publishers

Other Leading-Edge Books
from Berrett-Koehler Publishers

A Simpler Way
Margaret J. Wheatley and Myron Kellner-Rogers

Leadership and the New Science
Discovering Order in a Chaotic World
Completely Revised and Expanded
Margaret J. Wheatley

The Path of Least Resistance for Managers
Designing Organizations to Succeed
Robert Fritz

Rewiring the Corporate Brain
Using the New Science to Rethink How We Structure
and Lead Organizations
Danah Zohar

Complexity and Creativity in Organizations
Ralph D. Stacey

Images of Organization—The Executive Edition
Gareth Morgan

Imaginization
New Mindsets for Seeing, Organizing, and Managing
Gareth Morgan

Smart Thinking for Crazy Times
The Art of Soving the Right Problems
Ian Mitroff

Fusion Leadership
Unlocking the Subtle Forces That Change People and Organizations
Richard L. Daft and Robert H. Lengel

The Stirring of Soul in the Workplace
Alan Briskin

● ● ● ● ● ● ● ● ● ● ● ● ● ● ●

Available at your favorite bookstore,
or order directly from Berrett-Koehler:

On our website www.bkconnection.com

Or by phone 800-929-2929
Toll-free, 7 am to 12 Midnight Eastern Standard Time,
7 days a week (U.S. only)